Antigone in Ferguson
A Journey Through the Transformative Power of Music

Dr. Philip A. Woodmore

Editing by P. Woodmore Music Editing Team
Cover Design by Steve Hartman

Published by P. Woodmore Music
phil@pwoodmoremusic.com
www.philipawoodmore.com

ISBN: 978-0-578-78629-2

DEDICATION

Rest in Power, Michael Brown
You were an amazing young man taken from us too soon

CONTENTS

ACKNOWLEDGMENTS

I have been blessed with a younger blood brother, Daniel, to share this extraordinary journey in life with me! He reminds me that a video recording presently has irrefutable value in revealing what is not being written in police reports and brings awareness to the ever-increasing violence inflicted upon victims of every race.

It has been a tremendous journey to work with and learn from Bryan Doerries, Marjolaine Goldsmith, Teese Gohl and the team. I am so grateful for their support and friendship, as I ventured from the classroom to composition and performance across the globe.

I have been so blessed to have an amazing support team around me for this entire process! First, I would like to thank the board of the Phil Woodmore Singers: De-Andrea Blaylock-Johnson (assistant director), De-Rance Blaylock (board member), Duane Foster (choir manager), Latricia Allen (community engagement), John Leggette (outreach/event planner), Robert Crenshaw (assistant to the director) and Gheremi Clay (social media chair), for all their continued support, as I build my brand and promote the arts across this country.

I would also like to thank my new executive assistant, Daniel McRath, who has filled in the gap during the pandemic and helped me, as I created my in-home voice studio and moved my business to a virtual platform. I wish him well, as he pursues his master's degree and shares his gifts with the world. Special thanks to my former executive assistant, Robert Crenshaw, who allowed me to work in my creativity during the years I was juggling the classroom and touring the country, wishing him well, as he pursues his acting career.

Special thank you to my parents, Alma & Willie Woodmore, who have given me a phenomenal blueprint of life and have supported my dream of arts education every step of the way, and to my grandmother, Mamie Woodmore, (1921-2015) who was my biggest fan until her death. To Aunt Sarah, Aunt Mavis and Uncle John, Uncle Preston and Aunt Freddie for your life-long love and support.

To Isaac and Cecelia Brooks (1938-2020) my Godparents and lifelong support system, Pastor Peter and Geraldine McCreary, another lifelong support system, Virginia Dulaney-Cane (Mom #2), and Emily and Ian Kuykendall (my Godchildren).

To Nick Kuykendall, Jim Stine, and Andrew Yee for your continued loyalty and lifelong friendship.

To Joshua and Daniel Bristow, who spoke honest truths to me during this process to allow me to see a different perspective.

To Jordan Andes, Randal Herndon, Khalid McGhee and Joshua Moore, for being there as I pursue my dreams.

Outside of my team, many people have been in my corner for the past 20 years: Shawna Flanigan (COCA), Dr. Kathy Bowers (1948-2020) (Webster University), Michael Beatty (NYC mentor/friend), Beth Chesterton (Ignite Method), Dr. Wendy Sims (Mizzou), Jill Schuelen (former administrator), Grace Austin (colleague/friend), Marcelle Lashley-Davies (NYC performer), Rachel Chanoff (THE OFFICE), Catherine DeGennaro (THE OFFICE), Dominic Dupont (Theater of War Productions), Lisa Feder-Feitel (Theater of War Productions), Chris Page-Sanders (colleague/friend), Dr. David Clark (Saint Louis University), Bob Wilhite (colleague/friend), my Crestview family, COCA family, and my St. Louis Metropolitan Police Department Choir family.

To New Hope Baptist Church family, Union Baptist Church family, Outpost Church family, First Baptist Church of Chesterfield family, Trinity Community Church family and all those who shared an encouraging word along the way.

Thank you from the depths of my heart for your love and support!

FORWARD

After experiencing hundreds of *Antigone in Ferguson* performances, having the distinct privilege of hearing the stories of thousands of audience members and interviewing seven of the chorus members, writing this book has been a labor of love. It was my heart's desire to share some of these amazing stories with the world and even more so, give the reader an in-depth look into the creation and experience of *Antigone in Ferguson*. I invite you to soak in the love and humanity poured into these pages, experience the intensive process that emerged to create the music and the deep connection this project has to the tragedies of the killing of unarmed people of color.

As you explore this book, take notes, question things and reflect on how the topics may impact your life, and also your surrounding communities. After you read this book, share it with a friend. Let's work together to continue the necessary conversation of what it means to be human through the lens of the arts in hopes of making genuine progress. This book makes no attempt to thoroughly provide answers to this complex problem; it simply provides a framework to help shape your thinking and offers the universal language of the arts to provide context for these challenging topics.

There are two versions of this book: Edition one provides discussion questions at the end for personal or social reflection. Edition two includes an additional comprehensive study guide. This study guide focuses specifically on the music composed for the show to provide a framework to discuss the show and the music in-depth in an education setting. In addition, I have used lyrics from the songs in this production to develop questions that can be used to address many legal issues regarding justice in our country. The beauty of this study guide is that it can be used in the choral classroom, drama classroom, English classroom, history classroom and any classes where law, order and justice may be discussed. Teachers need creative and effective ways to breach this conversation with their students, and this study guide provides an artistic context for this challenging but necessary conversation. Furthermore, you might want to dig deeper into your own exploration and find the study guide useful in your own personal journey. Thank you so much for investing in this movement and this book.

Much love to the Brown, Head and McSpadden families and your continued struggle in justice for Mike. Thank you for continuing to share your son's memory with the world, as it is helping to shape the growing national conversation over the past six years and beyond.

We will continue to say their names,

Dr. Philip A. Woodmore

We the people,

As many celebrated 200 years of the life and legacy of Frederick Douglass, on March 18, 2018, I represented Theater of War Production by composing an original score to the Frederick Douglass speech given at the National Convention of Colored Men at Louisville, KY, on September 24, 1883. This presentation titled *Frederick Douglass on Staten Island* was performed at Temple Israel Reform Congregation in Staten Island, New York, for the Frederick Douglass Bicentennial. It had been 200 years since his birth. Honoring Mr. Douglass with my original work on Staten Island is another memorable highlight not to be forgotten.

Mr. Douglass's determined face was the face of freedom in his era. He was an abolitionist, orator and speaker for human and women's rights. He was so recognized that he made the history books.

My heart and mind imagined what he would say about our more perfect union today, or our current life, liberty and pursuit of happiness, as it exists for all people. While democracy is an ongoing work and will never be complete, we must be adherently careful not to turn back the hands of time.

"Without a struggle, there can be no progress."
~Frederick Douglass

Many of the mistakes of the past we cannot go back and redo, but we can start today to make a hopeful future for our children based on fairness and love—not hate.

In love,

Dr. Philip A. Woodmore

PREFACE

One humid summer morning in 2016, I rushed around the house, tossing everything I needed into a carry-on bag for a flight to Florida. Five days of beachside recovery, before the start of another academic year with my 300+ singers at Crestview Middle School (CMS), was exactly what I needed. The majority of my summer vacation had been spent directing a musical and teaching summer camps to eager performers at the Center of Creative Arts (COCA) in University City, Missouri. As I was rushing out the door to make my flight, my phone rang—it was COCA. Even though I did not have time to tackle whatever might be going on at that moment, I decided to answer the phone anyway.

On the other end was Christy Bertelson, chief speech writer to then Missouri Governor Jay Nixon, who wanted to connect me with her friend, Bryan Doerries, artistic director of Theater of War Productions (TOWP)—a social justice theater company that had been performing social-impact theater all over the world. She explained that Bryan was putting together a project for the St. Louis community and needed a local choir director for the collaboration. He was hoping to include police officers in this choir, among other community members, and was made aware that I was the St. Louis Metropolitan Police Department choir director. He wanted to discuss integrating the choir into an adaptation of Antigone, an ancient Greek tragedy by Sophocles, that Bryan had titled *Antigone in Ferguson*. I was intrigued but in a hurry. I asked Christy to give Bryan my number and tell him to call me the next day after I got settled in Florida.

Upon arrival in Florida, I caught up with my host family at their beach condo to relax and recharge. Bryan called the next day and introduced himself and explained all his ideas about the project. He aimed to create a choir of singers who held diverse views on challenging topics yet would collaborate to sing the choruses of Sophocles's Antigone. I assumed *Antigone in Ferguson* was already a musical work for which I was just organizing a choir; however, this was not the case.

I was asked to collaborate in the music writing process and form a choir to learn the music for the show. However, the conversation took an unexpected turn when he asked if I would like to be the sole composer of a full music score, to which I laughed. I had never done this before and did not think I had the wherewithal to complete this creative task. Bryan was calm and expressed his full confidence in me. I, on the other hand...well, let's just say that was the beginning of *Antigone in Ferguson*.

Antigone in Ferguson is a provocative theatrical hybrid using Greek tragedy with multigenre music and social justice conversations that often elicits strong emotional responses to sensitive themes, such as racialized violence, misogyny and suicide. The structure of the production creates a platform for audience members, who identify with the play's societal issues, to have a voice in the post-production conversation. *Antigone in Ferguson* was birthed from the racially-charged murder of a talented young man named Michael Orlandus Darrion Brown from Ferguson, Missouri.

Even before the murders of Eric Garner and Michael Brown in 2014, Black American citizens have been tortured, lynched and killed in horrendous, racially-motivated hate crimes. We have been harassed, lied on and murdered by the White gaze; corrupt police officers and self-proclaimed "defenders" of the law. Tragedies like these date back to the murder of 14-year-old Emmett Till in 1955, spanning to the well-known murder of 17-year-old Trayvon Martin in 2012, and have been ongoing through present day. As I finished writing this book, America was stricken once again with a string of unjust murders of Black Americans in our community: Ahmaud Arbery, Breonna Taylor, George Floyd, and Walter Wallace Jr., to name only a few.

With this perpetual cycle of hatred, violence, murder and injustice around the world and in my hometown of St. Louis, *Antigone in Ferguson* has become a poignantly relevant piece of art which can be used to progress the much-needed international conversation surrounding the evils of racism, classism and sexism. It is critical, now more than ever, that we amplify our voices to bear witness to the reality of these truths to help guide the consciousness of our citizens, especially from our White American allies, to advance the mission for needed change in the United States of America. It is extremely important to amplify the voices of the marginalized and silenced communities in our nation, as established powers (law enforcement, medical, media, law and policymakers, among others) too often abuse their positions of influence and manipulate facts in order to change the public perception of current events.

In this book, I will carefully examine the genesis of the *Antigone in Ferguson* project and its music in an effort for the reader to realize the power of saying "yes" to what may seem impossible. I will also reflect upon the development of my artistry, passionate musicianship, composition and music education practices while introducing the mentors and experiences that have shaped me as a musician, businessman and leader. Ultimately, I will share what it is like to experience *Antigone in Ferguson*, the creative process of its music and its impact on the world.

CHAPTER 1
Ancient to Present Tragedy

Antigone in Ferguson was birthed from a wild hunch that an
ancient Greek play about a teenage girl who puts everything
on the line in service of a law she believes to be greater than
the law of the state—the law of love—would resonate with
people living in Ferguson, Missouri, and in other
communities that have become synonymous with Ferguson,
through incidents of police brutality and racialized violence,
all across the country and the world.
    ~Bryan Doerries, director

Antigone in Ferguson has been a critical piece of art in the conversation
surrounding social justice since its conception in 2016. *Antigone in
Ferguson* was conceived with a creative and smart young man in mind,
Michael Brown, a graduate of the Normandy School District who was
headed to college in the fall of 2014. Along with so many other young
people, he was enjoying his summer with his friends before college,
unaware that his life—or rather, his death—would shake our nation.

On August 9, 2014, in Ferguson, Missouri, a sparse suburb of
St. Louis, the eighteen-year-old Black student was shot and killed by
Ferguson Police Officer Darren Wilson. Brown's body remained lying
on the street in the intense summer heat for nearly five hours. As a
result of the murder of an unarmed Black youth, a gathering turned
into protests marked by daily demonstrations and violent
confrontations with armed local police which brought national
attention to this horrific scene and the city of Ferguson.

You might ask, "Why use the play *Antigone* to draw parallels to
what happened on the streets of Ferguson?" In the words of the artistic
director of Theater of War Productions, Bryan Doerries, "It is not our
job as the staff to interpret the play for you, but for you as the audience
to respond to the play as you are experiencing it."

In the ancient Greek play, Polynices leads a bloody siege
against his native land, Thebes, and his brother, Eteocles. The two
brothers kill each other in battle, fulfilling a prophecy made by their
father, Oedipus, before his death. Antigone, the sister of Polynices and

Eteocles, informs another sister, Ismene, that King Creon, their uncle, has ordered Eteocles (who died defending the city) to be buried with full honors while Polynices (who was considered a traitor to the city) was to be left unburied for his body to rot. Creon decrees that anyone who attempts to bury Polynices will be condemned to death. Antigone, unsettled by her uncle's decree, does what she thinks is right for her brother and buries his body. She is caught in the act and then sentenced to death by being sealed alive in a tomb.

Haemon, Creon's son and Antigone's fiancé, begs his father to reconsider Antigone's punishment. But after Creon demonstrates that he will not waver from his decision, Haemon leaves in anguish to rescue his bride. Many try to convince Creon of his wrongdoing, including the blind prophet, Tiresias. Tiresias warns the king that his refusal to bury Polynices will bring the curse of the gods down upon his offspring within a matter of hours. Since the chorus knows that the prophet's words come true, the concerned citizens of Thebes plead with Creon to change his mind. Creon decides to free Antigone.

However, his decision comes too late. Antigone has already hanged herself. Haemon finds her body, considers the situation helpless and commits suicide. Creon then returns to the palace with his son's corpse to hear the news that after his wife heard of her son's death, she cursed Creon for the misery his pride had caused, and she also committed suicide. Left with nothing, Creon accepts responsibility for all of the tragedy he has caused and prays for a quick death. The play ends with a warning from a chorus member declaring, "The grand words of proud men are punished with great blows. That is wisdom."

When Michael Brown was murdered and turmoil followed, Bryan Doerries was moved to do something to help. He wanted to use his discussion-based theater as a model to create discourse and healing. Doerries is a writer, director, translator and self-described evangelist for ancient stories and their relevance to life today. He had spent the last six years of his career building a theater company that amplified the insights and perspectives of audience members who are closest to the social issues the company seeks to address by placing community-driven discussions at the center of the model, not as a talkback, but as an integral part of each performance.

His premiere project was *Theater of War*, a translated version of scenes from the Sophocles play, *Ajax*, a story of the journey of the great Greek warrior. Bryan discovered how he "stumbled onto something great" in his first translated work of *Ajax*, which was performed on a military base for officers and their spouses. Following the dramatic reading, service members and their families were invited and empowered to speak their truths in an organic way without fear of judgment or the need to disclose their current life challenges. Since the premiere of *Theater of War*, Bryan has toured his performances around the globe, using theater to spark necessary conversations around the themes presented in an effort to help bring healing to communities. He used the success of that production to create and name his company Theater of War Productions.

After forming the company, Bryan presented a theatrical reading of excerpts from the biblical book of *Job*, for the people of Joplin, Missouri, in the aftermath of the tornado that destroyed most of their town in 2011. The book of *Job* is about a wealthy man, living in a land called Uz with his family and all of his possessions, who was met with tremendous loss in his life. After losing it all, he did not curse God. The reading was presented as a way for residents to make connections to their own experience, assess their circumstances and begin a healing process from the trauma.

After the tragic death of Michael Brown and the uproar of the grieving community of Ferguson, Bryan sought to make deeper connections between the play *Antigone* and the community by involving music in the project. He needed a composer to score the music for his concept of theater. This was the start of our prolific friendship and business collaboration.

CHAPTER 2
Becoming an Artist: Phil Woodmore

"For You formed my inward parts; You wove me in
my mother's womb. I will give thanks to You, for I am
fearfully and wonderfully made; Wonderful are Your
works, and my soul knows it very well."
~Psalm 139:13-14, *New American Standard Bible*

My journey as a musician and composer began on October 19, 1981,
1:54 PM when Alma and Willie Woodmore welcomed me into the
world at Barnes-Jewish Hospital in St. Louis, Missouri. From early in
my life, my supportive parents witnessed my connection to music. All
of my life's work in music—academically, professionally and in
ministry—has prepared me for such a task as composing *Antigone in
Ferguson* and beyond.

My first music instrument, at one week old, was a toy guitar
that was half my body length. My parents were amazed that at eleven
months of age, I crawled to my mom's Baldwin piano in our home in
Chesterfield, Missouri (which now resides in my in-home teaching
studio), and pulled myself up beside the piano seat to find those
beautiful piano keys above my head. In preschool, my four-year-old
class sang Christmas carols for the entire school. I marched in and
placed myself on the front row, so I could easily see my family. I stood
very still and scanned the audience, seeing all White families, no sight
of my mom and brother. Someone had died at the church where my
father was the pastor, and my mom, First Lady Alma Woodmore, was
late getting to my performance because she was requested in a special
capacity at the church. After hurriedly driving to my performance from
the church, someone saw her running across the parking lot with my
baby brother in her arms to try and make it inside the performance hall
before they closed the doors. On the way over, my mom continually
said to my little brother, Dan, how disappointed I was going to be if
they missed the performance because they would probably not be
allowed in. But after thanking the person holding the door, she quickly
found a seat in the back row as quietly as possible, and as the

performance was about to begin, my brother yelled out, "Phil, we are here!" I gave a big smile, and we began singing "Silent Night."

Many nights prior to dinner, I would have the family sit in the living room for a family music session with me directing them in singing. So, there was no question that at the impressionable age of five, my parents would support my curiosity for music and enroll me into the Townsend Piano School in Ballwin, Missouri, with Sallie and Timothy Townsend (a piano school run by a wonderful mother-and-son team). I was not the best student, but I persisted for ten years and developed excellent sight-reading ability, keyboarding skills, music theory and aural skills. My passion and adeptness at music was refined, and I took up the identity as a musician.

At age 15, I applied and was accepted at the University of Missouri-Columbia (Mizzou) for a piano apprenticeship with master artist, Bernadette Randall. Bernadette, a Black woman who was an internationally renowned and accomplished musician, was a classically trained pianist and gospel artist. Ms. Randall was unable to fulfill her duties with the program, so she recommended Chester Andrews, a musician who lived in North County of St. Louis, who was available to help cultivate my growth musically and shape my craft. Chester mentored me on the particulars of playing gospel music for the Black church. Through this work, I developed improvisational skills and refined my ability to play by ear. Although I developed as a music reader and classical artist with ten years of classical training, there were disparate levels between my skill set and the demands of playing in the Black church. Subsequently, after a year of work with Chester Andrews, I decided to experiment with jazz studies to develop my improvisational skills. I enlisted the expertise of master artist Carolbeth True, who supported my acquisition of the language of jazz.

I am immensely grateful to my parents for recognizing my "music genius," as my mom would boast to my dad. My parents nurtured my love and talent for music before I knew how to express it. They not only accepted my creativity as a child, but cultivated my musicianship, rather than ignoring my gifts or discouraging me from pursuing music.

In addition to music training, my father's work in the church was formative to my journey. When I was four years and four months old, my father was called to pastor Union Baptist Church in Chesterfield, Missouri. This is where I would meet the pianist and musical inspiration of my life, Doris Frazier. I attended the weekly choir rehearsals and was enamored with the brilliant instruction of Mrs. Frazier. If someone sang off-key or any flaw during the praise-and-worship part of service on Sunday mornings, she would stop in the middle of worship service and start the song again until it was right. I was in love with her musical knowledge and teaching style.

Then, when I was just seven and without my parent's prior knowledge, Mrs. Frazier called me to the piano during an evening service at Union Baptist Church to play her Steinway & Sons grand piano. Fearless and naïve, I walked to the piano and played for the entire congregation. To everyone's surprise, especially my parents, I played the piece with confidence and precision. Her faith in my ability as a musician and confidence in my performance gave me the confidence to conquer this instrument and inspired me to continue practicing. Mrs. Frazier officially gave me a start as a church musician.

At the age of nine, I started playing the piano for my father's second church assignment in St. Louis, Abiding Branch Community Church (ABCC), a congregation he founded in his basement, but that expanded rapidly. I began playing hymns for the congregation and was the musician for the church choir. I have supported my father's pastoral work by leading and coordinating a music ministry in several churches in the greater St. Louis area while pursuing a professional career in music education.

Even as a teenage Black male, raised in an upper-middle class home by two loving parents, I have still experienced the fear of being pulled over by a police officer, uncertain about his intentions and the outcome. In Kenneth Meeks's book, *Driving While Black*[1], he provides a thorough definition of racial profiling that extends beyond our

---

[1] Meeks, K. (2010). *Driving while Black: Highways, shopping malls, taxi cabs, sidewalks: How to fight back if you are a victim of racial profiling.* Broadway Books.

highways and explains how to manage emotions and behavior during encounters with the police and others. Resources like Meeks's book are helpful for communities of color to prepare themselves for unfortunate profiling situations if they occur. While a help, it is unfortunate that books like his are critical for young men and women of color, as we try to navigate traumatic situations with law enforcement. Furthermore, communities of callous people in a racist system do not afford the decency of support, acknowledgment or fair treatment of people of color.

Another eye-opening phase of my journey was in the classroom at St. Louis University (SLU), where I was one of the few students of color in my college business classes. On many occasions during my time as an undergraduate at SLU in the dual major of business marketing and music vocal performance, I was singled out as the diversity quota for the department and asked to speak for all people of color in matters of race discussed in many of my business classes. There were occasions when I was treated as though the material was too difficult for me to learn and was even offered unsolicited help. I enjoyed my time at SLU, building lifelong friendships and discovering many things about my talents and gifts, such as the leadership skills I developed while running the SLU Gospel Choir and serving on the Black Student Alliance Executive Board. However, it is a sad truth that even in institutions of higher learning, Black Americans still experience stereotypical bias and often overt racism!

After graduating from college in 2005, I began my journey as a Black male educator in the Ferguson-Florissant School District, teaching middle school choir at two different middle schools. This was the result of a phone call from my colleague Doug Erwin, theater director at McCluer High School, who offered me a position teaching choir at Ferguson and Berkley Middle Schools. I had presumed my career path would be in business, but after contemplating the opportunity of a teaching position, I decided to give teaching a try. Having considered that my skill set would be better suited for high school and not middle school choir, I regarded this first position as a stepping stone to a different position in the next few years, if I could find a good rhythm in this career. It was inconceivable to me at the time that these middle schoolers in Ferguson-Florissant would teach me the greatest lessons I would learn in life. This decision to teach inevitably changed my life for the better.

The first semester was enlightening, as I quickly learned the difficulty and challenge of motivating students to do their schoolwork. On top of finding my way in the classroom, these schools had a different dynamic than I was accustomed to; Ferguson-Florissant had a larger percentage of students of color. As a novice teacher, I had to quickly learn how to service my students effectively. If the students are not focused or provided with a structured environment, some could be a hindrance to the classroom and obstruct learning.

I wanted to encourage the students to write, so I assigned them a writing assignment every morning. I asked them to create a journal with a log of words and quotes each day. They also compiled work on theory, poetry, history and other pertinent coursework to supplement their education to be successful musicians.

During my time in Ferguson-Florissant, I had the opportunity to work with and learn from two phenomenal master teachers in the district, Ellenmarie Wilcock and Cheryl Walker, both Black women who have been educating and inspiring students in music for many years. Mrs. Wilcock was the very first music education specialist who mentored me and invited me and my students to McCluer High School to sing with her choirs for my very first school concert. Mrs. Wilcock trusted my musicianship and passion for music, as we co-created a collaborative concert between the middle and high school. This performance was a great success for the students and the community.

After a successful winter concert with the high school choirs and a semester of teaching experience, I started to feel more secure in my assignment at the middle school. However, I was struggling to forge deep connections with my students. Most of my time and energy was spent proving my ability to teach music skills while managing my classes. I quickly learned an invaluable lesson that students don't care about what you have to teach them until they know that you care about them. After winter break, I had renewed energy and organized my classroom to be much more productive. In retrospect, I attribute much of my success to my colleague, Dr. Shonta Smith. Dr. Smith gave me valuable advice on how to survive teaching and best organize my classroom for success. She taught language arts in the same classroom I used at Berkeley Middle School in the periods before and after me, and we established a daily check-in to discuss our day and strategies for more productive instruction. I was new to the district, and her mentorship provided me with a wealth of wisdom and knowledge to navigate music education. After intensive planning and work with my students in the spring semester, we decided as a group to host a spring concert with both schools. To make this joint concert engaging, the students and I devised some great ideas to create a little healthy competition: a spring "Battle of the Choirs" concert.

Hosting a "Battle of the Choirs" concert meant having both choir programs competing against each other in a friendly battle in which the teachers decided the winner. After announcing this, though, I got a lot of push back from the administration. They expressed concern over low attendance at the middle school concerts and suggested that hosting a concert my first year might be a bad idea. I was determined to prove them wrong. The students and I created a lively program for the community that everyone could enjoy. Students invited their favorite teachers to judge the event and worked hard to learn several songs to perform. The students were excited to compete for the BIG PRIZE—a pizza party the next day. To the surprise of the administrators and myself, over 500 people piled into the theater at McCluer South-Berkeley High School for this concert, and it was a huge success.

During my first-year teaching, I began the master's program at Webster University to become a certified music teacher and receive my master's in music education. Focusing on music education in my master's program gave me a new outlook on music and teaching. During my time at Webster, I was able to participate in many education courses that allowed me to grow as a musician and teacher. It is important to note that I only had one composition course during my graduate program, which served as the foundation for the music I eventually wrote for *Antigone in Ferguson*.

While in the Ferguson-Florissant School District, my dream was to return to my alma mater, Marquette High School (MHS), to teach choir with my mentor, Judi Jones, the now retired theater director at MHS. This opportunity arose in 2006, when I learned that the choir teacher at MHS was not returning for the 2006-2007 school year. Judi Jones contacted me as soon as the job was posted and recommended that I apply. Ultimately, the high school position was filled before I could finish my application, but the opportunity to teach at one of the middle schools set the stage for my career as an educator. Crestview Middle School was a flagship school in the Rockwood School District, and positions in this building were highly sought-after.

I was honored to be entrusted with the choir students at Crestview Middle School in 2006 and took my position and time there seriously, as I continued to build and grow a strong middle school choral program. Finding my way through the Rockwood School District system as a student myself provided me with a framework for music education. While in Rockwood, I felt it was my duty to specifically mentor young minority students in my building. I worked hard to encourage my students of color to focus on a pathway to success and teach them how to manage situations in life. I was passionate in this regard for every student who was under my care, but I was especially concerned that the students of color achieved their potential in a predominantly White, upper-middle-class school district.

I struggled to adjust at CMS. I left my two middle schools of 100 students at Ferguson-Florissant and was now being challenged with 235 kids. But I persevered and continued to learn and develop my craft over time. By year three, the program was increasingly successful, and the building principal at the time, Dr. Jim Wipke, approved a trip for a select choir to travel to New York City (NYC) to present a 30-minute concert at the Lincoln Center. I had the honor of taking a select choir of 50 students, and of these students just one of the sixth graders was Black. It was such a joy to take this student out of St. Louis for the first time, on a plane for the first time and performing in NYC for the first time.

I believe in the power of music education to help shape students into productive citizens who live fulfilling lives, and furthermore feel that music is an effective tool that may be used to bring harmony and unity to all communities. Therefore, in my classroom, I worked every day to inspire young people to make good decisions, be upstanding citizens and continue to actively acquire knowledge through music. Drawing from the work of John Dewey[2], I strived to build a democratic classroom and focused on community-building in my school in an effort to make students feel psychologically safe, encouraged to take up new challenges, express themselves honestly and thrive. However, after the tragic event of Michael Brown's murder, many of our students of color didn't know how to process their feelings and struggled in the classroom for many weeks or even months to make sense of the senseless event. I had a heart for social justice but didn't know how to affect change after the events in nearby Ferguson.

In my twelve years teaching at Crestview, I aimed to inspire and cultivate a love of music in over 3,000 students. I grew the choir program by over 100 students. In my last year at Crestview, my choir program consisted of 350 students: a Boys Choir of 100 boys, an after-school Honor Choir of 85 students, a 90-voice Treble Choir, a 120-voice Mixed Choir and a Sixth-Grade Choir of 135 students. My eyes were opened to how well I excelled at teaching after my first year in Ferguson-Florissant, but I realized that teaching was my calling during my twelve years at Crestview.

Music is my passion, and middle school music education is the niche in which I have found much respect and great success. Although the direction in which public education has moved is problematic for me, considering its emphasis on statistics and standardized testing, entering my classroom every day to show my students how much I care about their education and well-being was top priority for me every year. I quickly learned that middle schoolers were receptive to guidance and could change their path for the better. I saw many students completely turn their lives around because of the music programs and the arts programs at Crestview Middle School. One child in particular was struggling with depression and insecurities but always had a dream

---

[2] Dewey, J. (1923). *Democracy and education: An introduction to the philosophy of education.* Macmillan.

of singing in front of the entire school. As a part of a conversation I had with this student during her transition to middle school in sixth grade, she told me about this dream to sing in front of the school, but knew it would never be a reality. After three years of hard work in music choir class with me, her last year at Crestview, she found her public singing voice and was able to fulfill that dream by performing a duet with me in front of the school at-large, an audience of around 1,500 people.

Outside of Crestview, I also invested time in other educational settings by accompanying camps and musicals at the Center of Creative Arts (COCA) starting in 1999 as a senior in high school, with accomplished arts educator and administrator, Eileen Manganaro. After spending six years working at COCA during the summers and teaching classes, I approached the senior staff with a complaint: the music offerings were limited and disorganized. There was far more interest in vocal music than the institution had available. This complaint, however, became a window of opportunity to fill a need, and it became my new task at COCA. After six months of planning, writing a curriculum and developing a program, I launched their newly organized music program in 2007 and became their coordinator of the voice department in addition to my work at Crestview.

Along with the programming at COCA, I launched a music company for advanced students who I cultivated and developed, with my supervisor, Shawna Flanigan, that we named Allegro Music Company. The Allegro Music Company became the premiere music company at COCA, which I integrated into my weekly routine throughout the school year from 2008 to 2017. Along with the development of Allegro, Shawna and I worked hard to develop a musical theater program as well. It was my goal to use music to carry the emotional context and narrative elements of the shows we were producing, much like the music of *Antigone in Ferguson*.

In 2017, I decided to pass the torch at COCA to another great music educator, Charlie Mueller, in an effort to spend more time traveling with *Antigone in Ferguson*. One of the programs in which I collaborated to develop, and still remains an important part of my work, was a series of summer courses started in 2008 called *Acting the*

Song with master artist, Michael Beatty. *Acting the Song* is a week-long intensive workshop which prepares young actors for auditions, with an emphasis on connecting their acting technique to singing techniques. We focus intensively on acting first and encourage performers to explore their acting through singing.

Although I enjoyed encouraging youth to be upstanding citizens in and out of the classroom, there was still an unfulfilled yearning inside me to progress social justice matters. God knew my heart because in 2009, the St. Louis Metropolitan Police Department (SLMPD) was searching for a choir director to lead the charge of putting together a song to sing for the 2009 September 11th Remembrance Ceremony in downtown St. Louis at Kiener Plaza. Detective John Leggette contacted me and asked if I would be willing to direct the chorus in singing a version of "The Battle Hymn of the Republic," the song of the Union in the Civil War by Julia Ward-Howe. I agreed, and after several sessions, the group had achieved a high level of mastery with the piece and delivered a stellar performance at the 9/11 memorial service.

Following this performance, the police chief at the time, Dan Isom, named me the official director of the St. Louis Metropolitan Police Department Choir, and we began programming concerts around the St. Louis area that included appearances at police department events and citywide gatherings. It was an honor to serve with the SLMPD Choir from 2009-2016. During this season of my life, I worked to find ways to engage with the community and share music with others, besides my work at the middle school and COCA.

As I continued to grow my community outreach in music, I received another opportunity to share the good news with a different community in St. Louis that was later pivotal to the creation of *Antigone in Ferguson*. In the spring of 2013, I received a phone call from Rona Paden, a member of the music ministry at Fee Fee Baptist Church, was aiming to develop a summer music series around the genre of gospel music. I reached out to my list of people whom I had sung with in the past to form a group of singers and musicians I called, "Phil Woodmore and Friends." Among these singers were several of my voice students, several members of the SLMPD Choir, members from

Trinity Community Church Choir, members of the Fee Fee Baptist Church Music Ministry and my good friends: De-Rance Blaylock and her sister, De-Andrea Blaylock-Johnson. It was an amazing worship experience to have all of these dear friends come together to make music; many of these singers would become the core of the *Antigone in Ferguson* choir. After this concert, I was striving for more opportunities to create music and engage with the community.

I decided early in my career that students need one-on-one mentorship and guidance to achieve a level of quality in their vocal training, music theory and aural skills; something I did not have growing up in middle and high school. Therefore, in 2006, I decided to open my own vocal studio in St. Louis and during this time, I was approached by many people, inquiring if I give voice lessons. Lacking experience in helping others to improve their singing, I continued to decline until one persistent mother convinced me that I would be the perfect mentor for her son. I finally relented and began coaching fifth grader, Jonathan Savage. After beginning this journey with Jonathan, I quickly acquired a few other students at Marquette High School, and before long, I was coaching 25 young people in the greater St. Louis area. Mentoring voice students became a passion of mine. I began preparing students for college auditions in musical theater, which quickly became one of my specialties. Since 2009, I have prepared over 150 students for college auditions, including creating a foundation to help students who needed financial assistance with lessons and resources to be successful for college auditions. Since then, I have coached well over 500 students privately—first in St. Louis and then expanding to Arizona and New York. Vocal coaching has become a strong niche for me and a large part of who I am as an educator.

One-on-one education provides a different outlet for students who need to express themselves in ways they are unable to express in a group setting. During my time coaching, I have prepared artists for *American Idol*, Broadway, *Cirque du Soleil*, *The Voice*, touring shows and local theater productions. Along with individuals, I have coached several casts of shows around St. Louis, as they do final preparation for their productions. All of these coaching opportunities of young students and professional performers prepared me to work with all of the theater, movie and television celebrities that would sing with the choirs of *Antigone in Ferguson.*

By this time in my career, I felt that I needed to continue my educational journey with a doctorate degree in music education. I wasn't ready to give up my position at Crestview Middle School nor my music program at COCA. I knew I did not want to stop teaching and was considering an online doctoral program; but thought if Mizzou would allow me to commute, I would consider making the sacrifice. After meeting Dr. Sims (who would later become my PhD mentor) and learning all about the wonderful opportunities at Mizzou, I was eager to apply and audition for a place in the choral and vocal departments.

My new journey towards a PhD at Mizzou began with participation in a summer choir program with Dr. Paul Crabb, among many other faculty members for my graduate music education courses. I then spent the next three years commuting—90 miles one way—between St. Louis and Columbia, on Tuesdays and Thursdays, to attend evening classes after teaching middle school students all day at Crestview Middle. Every summer, I participated in the summer choir on campus and enrolled in courses.

In 2013, I was reaching the tail end of my PhD program and had to take a one-year sabbatical from Rockwood to be a teaching assistant, to fulfill the residency requirement on campus for my in-service portion of the program. In that year, I taught a Basic Singing Skills course for the voice department, offered private voice lessons, served as a teaching assistant for the University Singers and worked with the university Concert Choir, all while teaching music and organizing choir tours and concerts for the university. I formed close relationships with new colleagues, one of whom became my good friend and mentee, Joshua Bristow, who contributed to the inspiration for one of the songs I wrote for *Antigone in Ferguson.* Another was an outstanding pianist and amazing singer named Khalid McGhee, who has accompanied many of my vocal and choral performances. Around the same time, David Jackson, another young man who changed my life for the better, shuffled into my Basic Singing class as a student in the spring semester, seeking help with a musical theater audition. After a few sessions and some generative conversation, David offered to assist me and help expand my business, P. Woodmore Music, LLC. Little did I know how much I would depend on him as I moved forward with my music career, large projects and the company I was building in the greater St. Louis area and, eventually, the nation.

Pursuing a doctoral program while teaching full time was no small feat, but it was an honor to persevere and emerge successful and inspired. In the beginning, my research interests included topics around the changing voices of adolescent male and female singers. Most of this interest derived from teaching middle school choir. I wanted everyone to feel comfortable in my classroom, yet one of the greatest struggles for pubescent middle school singers is dealing with their changing voices, especially the male voice. Adolescent males already grapple with the challenges of growing up, and having to deal with a changing voice in choir can be embarrassing to discuss. I spent three years at Mizzou studying the changing voice and the methods to support these young men to be successful choir singers through middle and high school. I was honored to author an article, "Support Middle School Boys through the Voice Change and They Will Continue to Support Our Choir Programs," published in the *Missouri School Music Magazine* in the fall of 2018. A change to my research topic, however, would soon occur after composing and experiencing the power of the *Antigone in Ferguson* performances with Theater of War Productions in 2016-2017.

CHAPTER 3
Building a Show from My Life's Work

"The power of the word, 'Yes!'"
~Dr. Philip A. Woodmore, music director

After attending the church where Michael Brown's funeral took place in 2014, Christy Bertelson, speech writer for then Missouri Governor Jay Nixon and friend of Bryan Doerries, called Bryan to inquire if he might have a project to help the Ferguson community find healing. Bryan initially declined this offer with doubts that his Brooklyn-based theater company would be effective on a local level in Ferguson.

Two years later in Brooklyn, New York, Bryan Doerries revisited *Antigone* and thought that a fresh adaptation of the play, with the title role played by a young woman of color and a chorus composed of diverse stakeholders from St. Louis, might bring healing to Ferguson. To be impactful in the community, he sought to build a Greek chorus[3] of local citizens who held diverse views on racialized violence, mental health and other critical issues facing society today. Therefore, Bryan hoped to create a "chorus that could not preach to itself" that included young people, members of the faith community, activists, concerned citizens and most critically, law enforcement. So, Bryan googled "St. Louis Police Choir" and found an article featuring a Christmas concert held at St. Louis City Hall with the St. Louis Metropolitan Police Department Choir that took place in 2010. After obtaining my name from that search, he received my contact information through COCA, which he relayed to his colleague, Bertelson, and requested that she reach out to me about the project.

By the summer of 2016, I was in the peak of my career as a music educator and was expanding my influence across the United States. Beyond managing a middle school choir program for 300+ students, I was also in full swing at COCA as voice coordinator and artistic director of the Allegro Music Company. Additionally, I was developing a gospel choir at Forest Park Community College called the

---

[3] Refer to Glossary for more information on a *Greek chorus*.

St. Louis Community Gospel Choir at Forest Park, flying back and forth to Northern Arizona University (NAU) working as the "Artist in Residence" for the state of Arizona while also directing the NAU Gospel Choir. I served as a vocal coach to over 50 students in St. Louis and New York—many of whom were preparing for college auditions in musical theater. I continued to serve as director of the St. Louis Metropolitan Police Department Choir, music director for three musicals at different high schools, all while progressing through my doctoral work at Mizzou.

How did we both know that everything we had experienced up to this point would lead us to make a production together that would impact lives and bring healing? We didn't. But we started with a simple conversation on August 5, 2016, while I vacationed in Florida, and he was in his apartment in Brooklyn. During our initial conversation, Bryan shared his vision for the project and his hope to include the SLMPD Choir and other members of the St. Louis community to form a democratic chorus of singers for this Greek tragedy. I assumed the music for *Antigone in Ferguson* was already written and that I would serve as the musical director, but Bryan informed me that the music had yet to be composed. He had approached his brother, Mark Doerries, professor of Sacred Music at Notre Dame University, who, in turn, had reached out to one of his graduate students who specialized in gospel music about collaborating on the project. After agreeing to collaborate with his brother on the music and organize singers for the project, I received the script from Bryan, and we spoke the next day to create a draft and talk specifics.

The next day, Bryan, equally excited, asked what I thought about the script. I shared my enthusiasm about the potential this project had and the need for such a model in our community. Shortly after this remark, Bryan informed me that he and Mark liked my resume so much that it became clear to them that I was the person to compose the gospel music for the show. I immediately laughed at what I perceived as an outlandish request. Bryan, however, responded with a long pause, probably unfazed by my remark. Not knowing how to interpret his silence, I shared my hesitations by explaining that my novice background in composition and the lack of time in my demanding schedule to take a project this enormous would be nearly impossible. I just didn't know if I could take on the stress of composing music for an entire show. He responded with, "You got this!" For reasons that were unclear at the time, Bryan had complete faith in me, which, in turn, gave me the motivation and a platform to begin this incredible journey.

With my vast network of musicians, I was confident that I could assemble a choir of singers for this event. Excited to get to work, I composed an email to 36 singers and musicians who would go on to represent the chorus in the first production of *Antigone in Ferguson*. Building on my success in St. Louis as a choral director, I was hopeful that many of the singers would consider participating in this amazing opportunity.

Even after agreeing to join the show, I still had reservations about Bryan asking for "gospel music" to accompany it. Being a man of faith and a minister of music in a church, I did not want to misrepresent the art form and tradition of gospel music, nor did I want to possibly shame the church by writing music that could be misinterpreted as disrespectful.

Immediately, I sought the advice of my father, a devout man of God and my spiritual leader. He and I have been working in the ministry together since I was eleven years old; he gave me my start as a minister of music and church choir director. Therefore, calling my father was the most sensible thing to do in making this decision. After a long discussion, he agreed that the message of the project was positive, and I should use my gifts and talents for this venture. Promptly, I called Bryan back and formally agreed to take on composing for the project. From there, *Antigone in Ferguson* was officially in motion.

It was August 6, 2016, and I had just agreed to write an entire musical score, find a choir and a band, teach them an unwritten musical score and share it with the entire St. Louis community on Saturday, September 17, 2016! I was overwhelmed with both anticipation and trepidation at the prospect of this new endeavor.

CHAPTER 4
Putting It All Together

The music is the driving force behind the story. It enhances the experience of the participants...The composer did a marvelous job of incorporating the musical traditions of Black Americans by including blues, jazz and gospel [genres] while also including other Western traditions such as the anthem and rock-ballad. [His] use of these styles...are intelligently used to reflect the mood at certain points in the story.
~Daniel McRath, tenor soloist

After Bryan called me in the midst of my break in Florida, I had to use all of my resources to get a choir together in 40 days. Where would I start?

In 2014, COCA celebrated 10 years of the musical theater program. From humble beginnings, our collaborative work grew until in the program's tenth year, we produced a 60-member cast of the musical, *Ragtime*. I had the opportunity to play the lead character, Coalhouse Walker, Jr., alongside a stellar cast. The cast and crew of COCA's 10th anniversary production of *Ragtime* was honored to have an original Broadway cast member of *Ragtime*, Duane Martin Foster, attend our production. After receiving a letter from Mr. Foster complementing our production and expressing his gratitude for bringing this work to St. Louis, I was certain I wanted to work with him and learn from his story and brilliant performance career.

The following summer Shawna Flanigan, COCA's director of arts education, and I decided to stage a production of *Memphis* the musical, which tells the story of a White man named DJ Huey Calhoun and his mission to bring soul music to a White audience in the South during the 1950s.

Since *Memphis* is a thought-provoking production that considers racial matters much like *Ragtime*, I knew we needed a dynamic director with a vision for its impact. Instantly, I recommended Duane as an option; Shawna agreed and requested that I reach out to him. I was nervous to contact him, as this message would be unexpected, but I was hopeful that he would be open to discussing the opportunity. Immediately concluding my meeting with Shawna, I headed to the music studio to prepare for a class I was teaching at COCA when a voice stopped me, "Phil?"

I looked up, and Duane was sitting in front of a dance studio. He was at COCA attending a dance class with one of his students and was about to leave when I rounded the corner. I explained the coincidence and shared our vision for the project and desire for him to direct. He immediately agreed to collaborate on *Memphis*. This organic friendship and work relationship grew throughout the ebbs and flows of the *Memphis* rehearsal process. We assembled a remarkable cast and put on a vital production for the St. Louis community.

With his passion and background, I thought Duane would be the perfect asset to *Antigone in Ferguson*. I originally asked him to collaborate as an assistant director to which he replied, "No, but I will perform with you." I was honored that a man who has graced the stages of Broadway would consider my talent and work worthy of his performance. I thanked him for his trust in me.

I also contacted my good friend De-Rance Blaylock. I was well-acquainted with her musical talent, having known her since I was eighteen years old, when I directed the gospel choir at St. Louis University; we shared a mutual respect for our God-given talents. I shared with De-Rance that I was a part of a project honoring the life of Michael Brown, and before I could even disclose the details, she exclaimed, "Yes, I'm in!"

Having these two individuals on my team was phenomenal; they both had a direct impact on Michael Brown's education in the Normandy Schools Collaborative. Duane was Michael's middle school theater teacher, and De-Rance worked in the IT Department at Normandy High School while Michael was a student.

I needed to have the police department represented in the storytelling to create the kind of diverse, dynamic community voice that Bryan and I had discussed. So, I called Detective John Leggette to inquire if he would be interested in participating in this project. He immediately agreed. Gheremi Clay, a voice student whom I coached for two years, was the final component to complete the storytelling-soloists for the project.

After securing my soloists, I began assembling the choir. Naturally, I called on my contacts of like-minded musicians from the Phil Woodmore and Friends concert in 2013 and groups I'd led, including all members of the police department choir, several of my advanced students at COCA, the members of my church choir at Trinity Community Church and a few of my mentees. In addition to my contacts, Bryan invited members of the Wellspring Church Praise Team.

Eventually, twenty-four singers accepted my offer to perform in the project; and after getting the confirmations, I then started putting together a band for the production. With all of the gospel music elements interwoven into this show, a traditional gospel combination of instrumentalists with the Hammond B-3 organ leading the pack would be the best way to go. Along with the organ, I decided to support the band and lead the singers by playing the piano. Then, I added guitar, drums, and saxophone to round out the band. Four instrumentalists agreed to participate in this project; two (the organist and the saxophonist) were brothers out of a set of triplets who worked in law enforcement. The drummer was an educator at Normandy High School, and the lead guitarist was my father, Pastor Willie Woodmore. Once the soloists, chorus and band were confirmed, I began quickly working on the structural sketches for each song.

After the birth of *Antigone in Ferguson* in September of 2016, this new group grew into the professional touring choir called The Phil Woodmore Singers, a choral organization under the umbrella of P. Woodmore Music, LLC—the company I created to protect my work on *Antigone in Ferguson* as well as several other shows for Theater of War Productions.

During August 2016, I labored over writing songs for the production. When I look back now, I wonder how I did all of this in such a short time. But it shows how with experience, a deadline and God's grace, you can achieve great things.

The Music

When invited to take on this incredible task of composition, I drew on all of the musical experiences I have encountered throughout my life to inspire me. I began with an intensive script analysis of Bryan's translation of Sophocles's *Antigone* while on my vacation in Florida. This led to a lyric writing forum around the poetic writing of the Greek choruses in the play with the support of one of my trusted voice students and mentees, Jonathan Savage, whose family I was staying with in Florida.

I first focused on the lyrics, as I read the script several times to gain a sense of the arc of the story to determine how the songs would complement the action on stage. The script contained five sections of poetry to be recited by the Greek chorus throughout the show; this was intended to add context and move the story forward.

I used the poetry to capture the key messages that would provide a through-line[4] to the story. Once I had organized my thoughts on the poems, I collaborated with Jonathan to start creating the lyrics to the five songs which came to be entitled: "Oh Light of the Sun," "Oh the World," "Destiny," "Oh, Love Invincible!" and "Purify the City."

When I returned to St. Louis, I charted my music in a music notation software. I wasn't an expert with the software, so I viewed some tutorials and slowly scored my music for our first rehearsal which was quickly approaching! I also wrote out piano parts for each song. "Destiny " was nearly finished first because it came to me so quickly in a brainstorming session; I just needed to add an accompaniment for the choral section in the middle (which I envisioned as a jazz moment) and flesh out a few more moments in the opening recitative. [5] I was still unable to move on to "Oh, Love Invincible!" because I could not get the opening section out of my head until one night, a week later while watching television, a new melody line struck me like lightning. I ran to the piano to create the second half of "Oh, Love Invincible"

---

[4] Refer to the Glossary for further information on the term *through-line*
[5] Refer to the Glossary for further information on the term *recitative*

and decided to simply merge the two halves together through a tempo change.

While composing this music, I was also preparing for another year of teaching. I was doing my best to split my time between preparing for my students and finishing the show. The 2016 school year would be my twelfth year in the classroom, and by this point in my career, I had established a rock-solid routine for beginning the year. Having the largest middle school program in the district with over 300 students, I needed to make sure I was well prepared to receive all of my students and treat them all with respect and care from day one. With this in mind, I spent many hours in my classroom preparing journals, folder cubies, seating charts and all-things-music to make my first days with my students a success. I focused each year on a theme to center our time together in the choir program. I usually based this theme on something tangible, like rock stars, sports, Hollywood, New York—simple things that would excite the kids. This year, my theme happened to be emojis, which I used to decorate the classroom and provide a fun atmosphere for the kids. Furthermore, I usually had about 200 returning seventh and eighth graders who knew my routine and system for the classroom, but the 130 incoming sixth graders needed to be acclimated to the ways of CMS Choir. Therefore, I had to spend hours making sure the classroom and structure for the sixth graders was in place before the first day.

I returned to St. Louis two days before my first teacher meetings; I usually liked to get in my classroom one week before teacher meetings to work in my classroom without distractions. This only left me with two days before the crazy—Yikes! Playing double-duty was hard, particularly since I refused to let my students suffer because of *Antigone in Ferguson*, no matter how important the project was. Moreover, I wanted to offer my best work which led to many late nights at the piano and a ton of frustration when ideas were not flowing.

For anyone reading this book who considers themselves a non-creative, true art is not created in a vacuum, nor is it created in a brainstorm session—an artist needs to feel, to breathe. An artist needs to live in order to create beautiful work. Sometimes, this cannot happen on a time constraint nor under stressful situations.

The first day of school arrived—a day of the year I find even more exciting than Christmas! I enjoyed meeting all my new students and catching up with all my former ones. But the most important element of the first day of school was that the students received a fresh start. Those students who had tough years prior were always reminded by Mr. Woodmore that, "The summer is a reset. This is a new year and a new opportunity to prove yourself."

Per usual, the first week of choir class was a smash hit. The first day was always so exhausting—lots of high-fiving, smiles, laughter and high-energy pep talks that always led to a tuckered-out Mr. Woodmore at 2:22 PM. But nonetheless, the *Antigone in Ferguson* music awaited me. I spent each day that first week of school in my basement, working out melodies, finishing lyric passages, notating my work and creating musical moments in the songs.

The *Antigone in Ferguson* score was shaping up nicely with just one week to go until our first rehearsal. For a successful first rehearsal, it was imperative to have the cleanest version of the score printed and bound for 30 people, including information pertaining to performances, venues, follow-up rehearsals, etc. I became overwhelmed with the enormity of my responsibilities and decided not to continue working on a song I wanted to add as my own gift to audiences called "I'm Covered," a song that was not in the translated words of Sophocles.

I disclosed to Bryan that I did not believe I could complete the song in time. He supported my decision, and I continued to work feverishly to finish the numerous preparations for our first rehearsal. However, the beauty of this song and the testimony are that in my weakest hour and lowest point, when I was completely burnt out, God gave me the melody and remaining lyrics for this song during a classroom lesson at my middle school, just days before our first rehearsal.

Amongst the Greek chorus are a few leaders who guide the chorus, as they share their stories. With this in mind, I decided to set up the musical form of the show like an oratorio[6]—using soloists to do the majority of the storytelling for the audience and a chorus of singers to provide all the other musical elements. I began to hear different styles of music in my head to the lyrics and melody lines I was creating. Therefore, I decided the intended gospel music requested would now include other styles and genres of music.

For example, determining the newly created lyrics for the opening song, "Oh Light of the Sun," I found the lyrics to be extremely vivid and provide a lot of context for the story. So, I decided the opening song should be more about the storytelling than the music. With this in mind, I envisioned the music to be majestic and serve as a triumphant opening to the show, especially since we were retelling the story of a dramatic war scene. After putting together all these elements, I decided that the opening moment should be in the form of an anthem[7].

The second song was much more intimate and conversational due to the lyrics. Therefore, I wanted the music to reflect a conversation between a small group of friends. So, I chose a trio to tell the story in, "Oh the World."

The third song had two very distinctive parts. The opening passages filled in vital information to the story from the storytellers and needed to be presented in a very poignant way for the audience. Therefore, I chose a dramatic musical setting with two soloists to create a recitative section in this song prior to the entrance of the chorus. I chose jazz elements to create a juxtaposition from the opening recitative portion of "Destiny."

I wanted the fourth song to resemble an upbeat church medley with a majestic plea ending the piece. And finally, the fifth song was to resemble a musical theater number in celebration of purifying the city.

With these general goals and guidelines, I began shaping the music, beginning with the melody lines of each song. From the melody lines, I then created solo and chorus moments. During the chorus moments, I started fleshing out harmonies for the chorus, finally

---

[6] Refer to the Glossary for further information on the term *oratorio*
[7] Refer to the Glossary for further information on the term *anthem*

followed by instrumentation for the accompaniment. All of these elements worked in tandem during the music writing process, as I had ideas swirling in my head and needed to get them down on paper as quickly as possible. The refining of this music actually happened during the rehearsal process and the weeks following the premiere of the show. In such a short time frame, I created these five songs with lyrics inspired by the words of the great Sophocles and music fit to the specific moments in the story to create an atmosphere in the theater.

Oh Light of the Sun

When creating ideas for this song, I decided to begin with the opening line of the chorus, "Oh Light of the Sun," which I envisioned as an anthem. The storytelling in this piece is profound, so I gave some of the recitative moments to both the soloists and the choir throughout. As I read deeper into the text, I encountered a poetic retelling of the civil war between brothers, Polynices and Eteocles, who had just killed each other in battle fulfilling the curse of their father Oedipus.

With such vivid descriptions and text, I decided to paint the picture using mostly musical storytelling elements. I created a melody line for this piece first and then began to flesh out the moments for each soloist and then the ensemble. I wanted to begin with an instrumental fanfare[8], followed by a majestic opening choral moment from the chorus which would then lead into the soloists sharing more of the story with the audience. It went back into the chorus, "Then the battle turns in our favor," heralding the triumph of war, and then quickly turned to tragedy, as the brothers killed each other. I concluded the piece with the same fanfare in which it began but left the audience with a poignant message, "And may we never forget what happened here, and never go to war again."

This theme was so impactful to me, as I worked on the song, because it extends an encouragement to people in our society to learn from our history, stop repeating mistakes and begin enacting choices

---

[8] Refer to the Glossary for further information on the term *fanfare*

to make change. Too many times we are moving too fast to process what is actually happening in today's culture and society. Additionally, we do not always take the time to sit under the council and wisdom of those who have come before us to work on breaking these destructive cycles. This text must be a mantra for our society if we ever want to destroy the deep- rooted problems which oppress many of the citizens of this country.

"Oh Light of the Sun" comes after a private scene in which Ismene and Antigone contemplate what to do with the body of their dead brother, Polynices, who has been left lying on the ground after the civil war and has been declared by their uncle, King Creon, not to be worthy of burial. Antigone is wrestling with this issue because she knows it is not right to leave her family member lying unburied, regardless of the declaration of the King. As we come to the end of this conversation with Ismene and Antigone, in the distance, we hear the light patter of the drums in a militaristic fanfare, indicating the entrance of the Greek chorus. The drumming becomes louder and louder to give the visual of the Greek chorus getting closer to the town to describe the scene.

I titled this number "Oh Light of the Sun," which I envisioned as an anthem with a very dense homophonic[9] texture along with vibrant music and energetic vocal lines. This song opens the show and signals the entrance of the Greek chorus; therefore, I felt it appropriate to begin with the first theme, which I wrote as a fanfare played by the band. Following this fanfare, the choir joined in, repeating the theme in moments of eight-part harmony, which painted a picture for the audience of the civil war which had just ended in the play of this trilogy, *Oedipus at Colonus* (Sophocles, 401 B.C.E.).

Oedipus at Colonus is about the tragic hero's life, Oedipus, and his mythical significance for Athens. Oedipus goes through a transformation from being a beggar banished from the city into a figure with incredible power. The choir begins by sharing the story with the audience about the "light of the sun that graces the seven gated cities." This description of the light breaking over the horizon

---

[9]Refer to the Glossary for further information on the term *homophonic*

reminds me of the opening of Disney's *The Lion King*™ and the beauty of the earth on display, as the sun breaks. In this instance of *Antigone in Ferguson*, though, the light is shining on the aftermath of the civil war during which brothers Eteocles and Polynices killed each other. The story develops with two storytellers (a tenor and soprano) sharing details of the war for the audience. The chorus then informs the audience about the moment "the battle turns in our favor," which is presented in a soprano[10], alto[11], tenor[12] (SAT) gospel trio structure.

The SAT traditional gospel harmony is a trademark of the great Dr. Mattie Moss Clark, the mother of the Clark Sisters, and provides a unique sound using three-part harmony. The song shifts into a minor tonality, as the chorus discusses the tragic fight and death of the brothers and then ends with a restatement of the opening theme: victory in the war. The most striking moment in the opening is the final line, which simultaneously offers encouragement and warning to the chorus and audience. They share, "And may we never forget what happened here, and never go to war again." This moment is also written with an eight-part homophonic structure, but it is sung in the lower register of all voice parts, providing a more reflective afterthought, as the piece concludes. In the final moment of this song, the mezzo-soprano[13] storyteller reminisces one final time about the glorious light of the sun.

Oh the World

The second piece, "Oh the World," was actually the fourth song composed in the writing process. I had a vision for this piece but struggled to connect the text with a melody line. After some experimentation, I finally began to shape this song after returning to St. Louis from my vacation in Florida.

The song follows the opening number "Oh Light of the Sun," when King Creon emerges to speak to his constituents. He shares the

---

[10]Refer to the Glossary for further information on the term *soprano*
[11]Refer to the Glossary for further information on the term *alto*
[12]Refer to the Glossary for further information on the term *tenor*
[13]Refer to the Glossary for further information on the term *mezzo-soprano*

decree that Polynices (who came to burn the city down before he was stopped and killed) will be left unburied, and the punishment for anyone who violates this decree will be death. Antigone, Eteocles and Polynices's sister, refuses to follow the king's orders and buries her brother. A guard announces this news to the king who demands that the perpetrator of the crime needs to be produced.

Following this scene comes the second piece I wrote for this production, "Oh the World," which starts as a simple song between the saxophone and the soloist. The song begins with the saxophone introducing the melody line accompanied by the guitar; then, the baritone[14] storyteller joins in to share an enchanting tale about the beauty of humankind. This song celebrates the wonders of man: "He can heal the sick, lessen all the pain, even extend life, but death will still remain. The righteous who upholds nature, rides high through the city, but the righteous who are threatened are cast out without pity."

One of the extraordinary, unplanned elements of this show is the direct tie to the many themes of Christianity and sharing the "good news" or the "gospel" through the lens of Greek tragedy. One such moment is through the lyric, "He can heal the sick, lessen all the pain," which can be interpreted as Jesus healing the sick in the Bible.

To add more drama to this gospel trio, we added another layer to this piece, bringing in the chorus to lend support to the trio with the singing of background oohs and ahs followed by a proclamation from the chorus who sings text from the opening number, "Oh Light of the Sun." This provided a unique element to the second song, "Oh the World," by reminding the audience of what they learned from the first song, "Oh Light of the Sun."

After the climax of the song, which includes the ensemble and trio of "Oh the World," the storyteller reappears one last time to share about the wonders of the world, "But none more miraculous than man," followed by a concluding musical statement from the saxophone and the guitar to end the piece. This reflective song has

---

[14] Refer to the Glossary for further information on the term *baritone*

beautiful melody lines which allow for the listener to digest the text in a musical way.

Destiny

Before the song "Destiny," we witness an intense conversation between Antigone, Ismene and their uncle, King Creon, which ends with the king declaring Antigone and Ismene criminals and arresting them for Antigone's crime.

"Destiny" was envisioned as a dramatic recitative for the soloists. The text here is a strong reflective moment in the storytelling; in the first iteration, I decided the soloists should sing this piece entirely. After a deeper exploration of the opening passage, I decided to include the ensemble to create more of a light-hearted choral moment to balance the heavy text and dramatic singing of the opening recitative. The piece concludes with the baritone soloists sharing the final passage of the poetry, followed by a choral moment using a four-voice homophonic structure leading to a final chord with open fifths. I decided to use this writing style of open fifths in this moment because adding the third in the chord structure gives resolve. If we hear a major chord (creating happiness or comfort) or a minor chord (creating tension or stress) in the music, we will have some musical context in the final moment of this song. The deletion of the third in the chord structure leaves us without this answer which creates an open space in the music and therefore, causes suspense for the audience. These open fifths leave the audience unsettled about what is to come—the feeling of wonderment and curiosity lead the audience into the next scene. After workshopping this song several times, we arrived at the final version of the song described in the next paragraph.

"Destiny," in its final version, becomes a dramatic storytelling moment in the production. The song begins with a powerful recitative section performed by the mezzo-soprano soloist that conveys the impact of war amongst the ancient Greeks. The storyteller then laments over the killings occurring generation after generation, giving the audience pause on the impact of repeating mistakes over and over. Following this soul-stirring moment by the mezzo-soprano soloist, another storyteller then comes to tell us the tragedy of this family is destined by divulging that the house is cursed, and destiny's blade is coming for the royal family. Both of these storytellers then lead the chorus into a jazzy refrain, "The price of good fortune being calamity." Finally, the baritone storyteller joins in to remind us of fate and specifically, Antigone's destiny, by sharing the following text: "The humble man keeps his head down and remains alive and rides out the storm. Destiny can be avoided but cannot be escaped." After the baritone soloist shares with the chorus some details about Antigone's destiny, the chorus then reflects on this counsel at the end of the piece in a mystifying choral moment in the music. During this moment, the audience is allowed time to consider Antigone's destiny.

Oh, Love Invincible!

The fourth song, "Oh, Love Invincible!," was written in two segments. The opening section was simple for me to create, as I strove to produce an authentic old-time gospel feel for this number, created through a standard gospel progression with an upbeat tempo. After fleshing out this opening section, I was perplexed about the direction of the second half of the song, as I was hearing two different songs in my head that I wasn't sure would blend.

"Oh, Love Invincible!" has gone through many iterations since the beginning of this process. Stylistically, the song is an upbeat gospel song akin to what would be used during the offering portion of a traditional Black church service. In the tradition of the Black church, preachers often ask for "walking music" during the offering. This has become a standard part of the service in most churches, and even though we are not taking up an offering during the production of *Antigone in Ferguson*, the music represents this part of the show.

The beautiful symbolism of this offering music occurs during the moment in the show when the choir is pleading with the king to let Antigone live, advocating for her life. In the Black community, we support each other in very powerful ways, especially in the arts communities. Just as members of the chorus of *Antigone in Ferguson* formed special connections with each other throughout the process of learning and performing the music, during this moment in the show, the chorus undoubtedly pleads for Antigone's life and advocates for her in this same vigorous way.

"Oh, Love Invincible!" starts and ends with the strongest message in the show—love! A storyteller emerges and proclaims, "Oh, love invincible! Oldest and most powerful force in the universe. Almighty, I call out to you!" Following this proclamation, two members of the chorus come out and share a story with the choir and the audience. After the story, the choir then deliberates about love: "Love is good, love makes you mad, love is fleeting; love is sad. Love is ancient, transcending time, love is patient; love is kind."

After this deliberation, we transition from the upbeat "offering music" into a powerful gospel ballad which then becomes a plea to: "Let Antigone live!" The chorus implores, "Please, I pray to you, let Antigone live," which creates a boisterous moment for audience members, as the choir takes the role of intercession on Antigone's behalf, and for those who might not be people of faith, an opportunity to witness passion at its highest level. The song ends with a choral moment declaring that Antigone deserves to live because the act of burying her brother was an act of love, and she deserves to be treated mercifully.

Purify the City

The chorus is the voice of the people in the production and also represents the voice of reason for King Creon, as he deliberates Antigone's release. The chorus attempts to convince the king to release his niece, Antigone, several times throughout the production. The chorus tries one final time to sway the king's decree; he finally agrees to release Antigone and runs to free her. The chorus rejoices through the song, "Purify the City."

"Purify the City" is a song of celebration about the need for the community to cleanse society of its disease and corruption to "wash away the unholy pollution." This song was actually the second piece I wrote while in Florida. I discerned from the text that I wanted this to be an upbeat, celebratory, musical-theater-style feature in the show. I was so inspired by the concept that I composed the music in one sitting. I first built the opening recitative as a way of inviting the people of Thebes to listen to the great news about Antigone's release and impending marriage.

The storyteller enters exclaiming, "The people of Thebes call out to you!" followed by an introduction from the piano that leads the chorus into a spirited stanza encouraging the community to unite and work together to purge the city. The storyteller rejoins and proclaims the good news of Antigone's release and her opportunity to marry her love as well as the community uniting in love, not violence. The second half of this piece is a boisterous expression of joy. The choir continues to grow in liveliness and volume, using an inversion of the chords to build energy in the vocal lines. A grand musical theater punctuation, more commonly known as a button, ends the song, sharing the final proclamation, "Purify the City."

This song was my favorite during the writing process because it is exuberant throughout, but more importantly, offers a contrast to what will later occur when the chorus instantaneously falls silent by Antigone's dramatic death in the following scene. Musically, the piece was written as an upbeat musical theater number with gospel influences. I again used the three-part (SAT) gospel harmony in the ensemble intertwined with a leading soloist.

The beauty of this song is that it is a glorious celebration and genuine expression of joy, hope and progress. During this expression of joy, the king rushes to spare Antigone's life; he is too late. Before he arrives to save Antigone, she has already died an honorable death, which takes the form of suicide in this particular translation of the text. This halt in the celebration jars the audience, as they immediately hear the news of Antigone and Haemon's deaths due to the poor decision and timing of the king.

As the king returns to the city with his son's dead body, who had fallen on his own sword out of grief from Antigone's death, he gets the tragic news that his wife has also killed herself, and now the king has been left with nothing. One of the chorus members shares a poignant line with the king before he leaves the city in despair, "You have learned too late." Following the king's exit, the choir leaves the audience with a powerful gospel ballad, the song I almost couldn't finish. My tribute to the project, "I'm Covered," led by the incomparable praise and worship leader, De-Rance Blaylock, ends the show.

The Greek tragedy confronts the audience with moral dilemmas to contemplate, such as suicide, misogyny, corrupt government, racism, sexism and classism. The connections between the play Sophocles wrote thousands of years ago and what our society still deals with today are disheartening and tragic. However, works like *Antigone in Ferguson* face these themes and try to bring about change, one audience at a time. Audiences all over the country have responded to the work and reflected on how it has impacted their way of thinking and evoked change in their lifestyles. Later in the book, we will explore in detail some of these interactions with audiences and their heartfelt sharing and my personal reactions.

CHAPTER 5
Thank God, I'm Covered

No weapon forged against me shall prosper. / When
I'm in need, You're always there. / When the storms
of life are raging, / When the enemy surrounds me! /
My God will cover me. / When I'm in trouble, When
I'm lonely, / My God will cover me. / Oh, greater is
He who is in me / than he who is in the world!
~"I'm Covered" lyrics

After I agreed to take on the task of writing the music for *Antigone in Ferguson*, I immediately felt constrained by the agreed upon structure of the music. Being a creative person, I wanted the artistic freedom to express something from my heart that was not thematically a part of the play, but still offered something meaningful to the show. Within the first 24 hours of agreeing to take on this project, I called Bryan and asked if I could write something for the project that was solely my contribution. He agreed, and I immediately focused on creating a song to add to the production. I first considered all of the public servants, such as the police officers whom I directed in the police choir, who put themselves in harm's way every day for our community.

I then considered how we as a Black community in America are under attack every day and that we all need to be covered and protected. I reflected on the relationship I built with the St. Louis Metropolitan Police Department Choir over the past several years and was determined to write a piece to offer encouragement to my friends in the police choir and the community, as a means to move forward from the murder of Michael Brown and the protests that followed in Ferguson.

When I coordinated the Phil Woodmore and Friends concert at Fee Fee Baptist church two summers before I wrote the music for *Antigone in Ferguson*, I programmed a gospel piece, "Safety" by Oscar Williams Jr., which shares the powerful message of taking comfort in the safety of the arms of the Lord. Taking this message and my experience working with law enforcement, I created a song around the theme of being covered, and thus the concept for the song, "I'm Covered," was born.

Back in Florida, I created the lyrics to the chorus of "I'm Covered" before I returned to St. Louis. The overwhelming task of writing the five songs for *Antigone in Ferguson* consumed all of my mental capacities over the next 20 days, and I was uninspired to write any additional lyrics or compose any music for "I'm Covered" during the final days of music prep before our first rehearsal. I informed Bryan that I still wasn't confident in finishing the song before the show opened; it would be a better use of my time to focus on finalizing the other songs. He shared his gratitude for the work I had done and assured me we would complete the production successfully; "I'm Covered" could come later, meaning it could be written and used for other versions of the production.

With only days left until the first rehearsal for the choir, I was sitting at my desk during my planning period at school talking on the phone with one of my mentees, Josh Bristow, in Atlanta. I shared my frustration over my inability to make progress on "I'm Covered." He asked me what the issue was, and I shared with him that I had the lyrics for the chorus, but I wasn't connecting with anything for the verse.

After we conversed for a while, he relayed some lyrical options from the Bible. I strongly connected with 2 Samuel 22:1-4, in which David proclaims God's protection, the main theme of "I'm Covered."

> David sang to the Lord the words of this song when the Lord delivered him from the hand of all his enemies and from the hand of Saul. He said, "The Lord is my rock, my fortress and my deliverer; my God is my rock, in whom I take refuge, my shield and the horn of my salvation. He is my stronghold, my refuge and my savior—from violent people you save me. I called to the Lord, who is worthy of praise, and has been saved from my enemies." 2 Samuel 22:1-4, from the *New International Version Bible*.

After our conversation, I started my day with two sixth grade classes, followed by seventh grade Treble Choir, an all-girls choir class, before my 30-minute lunch break. When my seventh graders entered, we started class as usual with a sight-reading activity followed by a music theory lesson on the board before rehearsing their music. While delivering their theory lesson, having meditated on the verses that my mentee gave me for "I'm Covered," I began humming a melody line. As this melody started shaping, I then started hearing the music in my head; it resonated with my total being instantaneously. My reaction to this God-given music was so intense that I asked my assistant to take over the class, and I retreated to a practice room in my classroom and composed the song in 20 minutes.

I finished the last piece of *Antigone in Ferguson* days before the first rehearsal. After putting the song together, I completed the notation at home two days before our first rehearsal. In the final moments I was at the piano creating the accompaniment, I was singing the verse: "My God, my rock. In whom I trust, I take refuge in you. You are my shield, my savior. I will call upon the Lord, who is worthy to be praised. And He saves me from my enemies."

And suddenly, while I was singing the words, I became overwhelmed with emotion and began to cry. My first thought was that this was definitely God-inspired; I had no intention of finishing this song, yet He gave it to me in a manner of minutes. I could not have accomplished this task on my own; but also, I realized I was overwhelmed and emotionally exhausted from this 23-day process of writing music for Bryan's production. Little did I know that my response to the song while writing, would be the same reaction audiences around the world would have when it was performed.

After I finished "I'm Covered," I originally dedicated the song to the members of the St. Louis Metropolitan Police Department Choir who had been a great example for me of outstanding law enforcement officers serving the community and not tearing it apart. But, after observing audiences' responses and their encouragement of being covered, as we conquered life's challenges as a society, community, nation and tribe of thinkers, the song quickly turned into a universal message of hope for all communities and became a healing hymn for all people. To this day, I am overwhelmed at how the song speaks to people of all faiths, nationalities and backgrounds through the messages of the Scripture.

Originally, I introduced "I'm Covered" to the audience with a little setup about the background of the song to prepare them to listen to the song's message. In the beginning, I introduced the song from the keyboard, and then it grew into a choir member introducing it with a prepared speech about the universal nature of this song. Finally, when *Antigone in Ferguson* prepared for its run in New York, the speech was removed, and we connected "I'm Covered" directly to the action of the show.

After King Creon learns of all the tragedy that has occurred, he begins to cry out in anguish. The chorus doesn't say anything to the king's cry but supports him with a low hum. This hum comes from a tradition in the Black church as well; during prayer and other moments during service, the congregation and musicians support the pastor with background music to add to the unity in the room. Even though this king completely mishandled this situation, the Greek chorus still supports him in this way, as he leaves to try and abide with his wrong decisions.

After the king exits Thebes, the chorus then sings a beautiful bookend to the production by giving us a line from the opening number, "Oh Light of the Sun," bringing closure by ending with one of the most striking lines in the entire show, "And may we never forget what happened here, and never go to war again." This phrase has so many interpretations, and as a part of the Theater of War Productions model, we purposefully allow the audience to make its own interpretation of the ending. I remind the audience of that line in the song by beginning and ending the show with that musical phrase.

Following this bookend, there is a fluid transition into "I'm Covered" through the sopranos singing the final "again" as an afterthought, which gives space for the piano to introduce the new melody line. "I'm Covered" starts simply with a piano introduction establishing the melody and mood of the song. Following this moment, the voices are added singing the chorus as a unified front. The chorus of the song symbolizes unity amongst the chorus of people and also offers that same unity and strong hopeful message to the audience. Praise and worship leader, De-Rance Blaylock, leads the healing hymn in a soulful and spiritual way that uplifts the choir and the audience.

De-Rance Blaylock, a graduate of Normandy High School, has skillfully presented "I'm Covered" to audiences all over the world with passion and precision every time she graced the stage with her presence and powerful voice. I love when De-Rance is given the opportunity to share her story. She is a true warrior and is committed to everything that she does. She offers her own testimony:

"Hi, friend!" Those were the first words I heard when I answered my phone on a hot Saturday morning in August of 2016. I was sitting in the middle of my bed eating cereal while watching cartoons. I heard my phone ring and saw on the screen that it was Phil Woodmore.

Phil and I have known each other since 2001. He and my sister De-Andrea were co-directors of the Melody of Praise Gospel Ensemble (MOPGE) at St. Louis University. I would sometimes help with concerts as a guest director, guest soloist or mistress of ceremonies. Phil would later hire me as a voice teacher at the Center of the Creative Arts (COCA). During this time, we developed a friendship that would endure both beautiful ups and heavy downs in our lives. Because of this friendship and because of his work ethic, I became a huge fan of his.

That Saturday morning, I looked at the phone, and it was Phil calling. I answered my phone with a "Hey Phil!", and he responded, "Hi friend!"

Phil's response told me everything I needed to know: he's about to ask for a favor. We had a short talk for a moment, "How are you? How's your vacation?" etc. After the small chat, he began his spiel, "I received a call from a creative director in New York. He received my information from the governor's office and wants me to be a part of a big project that deals with social injustice and the events that occurred after Michael Brown's death. I was wondering..."

"YES!!!", I exclaimed. I was so excited that I didn't let him finish. I told him I would do whatever was needed from me. I didn't care about solos or features; I just wanted to be involved. I was willing to do anything for the awareness of the injustice surrounding the murder of Mike.

I am a former educator. I worked twelve years for the Normandy School District: six years at an elementary school and six years at the high school. I graduated from Normandy High School a long time ago, so working there was nostalgic. I enjoyed working with the staff and helping the students in any way that I could. During my last year of working there, I met a young man named Michael Brown. Mike was a pretty quiet kid, but he could make you laugh when he did speak. Mike would come into my office for various reasons. A lot of times, he would come in because he saw that I'd bought food. It wasn't because he was starving. It was because he was a kid who loved to eat, like every other kid.

August 9, 2014, changed my life. I came home from the beauty salon that afternoon, and I turned on my laptop. I logged onto Facebook, and the first thing I saw was the picture of Mike's body lying in the street. I didn't know that it was him at first. I did something that I regret: I zoomed in to see his face. When I realized it was Mike, I screamed. I tried to suppress my screams because I didn't want to scare my mama, who was downstairs.

Mike was about to head to college in a couple days, having graduated from high school. Mike had his whole future ahead of him, and yet, it was snatched from him within moments. I had stayed glued to my phone that weekend, talking to former coworkers and friends who lived out of town. I also stayed in my mama's bedroom and laid with her as she tried to console and comfort me. I had just lost one of my babies. When working in education, I was a firm believer that the students became my responsibility once they crossed the threshold of my classroom or office. Because of that, I called those students my babies. Michael Brown was one of my babies.

Two years later, I found myself sitting in the middle of my bed, listening to my friend Phil, as he continued giving me information about the Antigone project. "45 minutes of music in 30 days! Is he serious?" I remember blurting this out as Phil told me that he'd been given the challenge.

He confirmed and continued sharing his information. I told him that I would do some serious praying for him, and I was here if he needed anything. We ended the conversation, and I returned to watching the cartoon, *Daria*.

A couple weeks later, we were sitting in a choir room on the Forest Park Community College campus. Phil introduced me to a song titled, "I'm Covered," after most of the choir left. He started playing the song and introduced the melody for the solo. I told him it was nice. However, I suggested that we start the solo an octave lower. Phil was going to sing the solo originally, so he wrote the solo for himself in his tessitura[15]. By God's providence, he decided to pass the song to me. In our first rehearsal, he sang the solo to me and asked me to move the pitches for the solo up an octave in the alto/soprano range. I told him that

---

[15] Refer to the Glossary for further information on the term *tessitura*

was great, but I was going to bring it back down to where it was. After our first rehearsal, I sat with the song for a few days and made a few tweaks to the solo and then was ready to perform at our first show at Normandy High School.

After the third performance of the day at the former Wellspring Church in Ferguson, we realized what kind of beast the song was going to be. It touched anyone who heard it, including myself. Every time I sing, "I'm Covered," I continue to offer a sense of hope and strength. I also continue to use my voice as a covering for Mike's body. I couldn't do it physically, but I can try to cover him figuratively and display his humanity through song.

I thank God that Phil gave me the opportunity to sing his beautiful songs. He could've chosen anyone else to sing. He could have sung it himself. Instead, he gave me the responsibility to minister his words to people all around the world, and I do not take that for granted. I am eternally grateful, and I will always be his friend and fan.

De-Rance Blaylock has been part of this production since day one and has only missed one production (out of the several hundred we have performed over the past four years) to attend her grandfather's funeral. This remarkable woman has shared her heart with thousands of people through this incredible song and has single-handedly transformed lives through her voice. One evening, during the run at the St. Ann and Holy Trinity Episcopal Church in Brooklyn, New York, a man stood during the post-performance discussion and shared a story with us. He had a weak voice and was speaking slowly, but we soon learned why:

I didn't get to see the entire show, but I was walking down the street and heard this voice singing the last song, and I was just drawn in here to see what was going on. I had a stroke a while back and haven't spoken publicly since, but had to come in here to see what was going on and tell you all this story.

This is one of many stories shared during this process that became a direct confirmation to me that the music and its performance create a power that people can feel. Tears immediately rolled down De-Rance's cheeks and the faces of many other choir members when they heard his testimony. Our choir repeatedly experienced the power of music and how it speaks a universal language that nothing else can. De-Rance's masterful vocalizing along with her spiritual and authentic presentation of the text has given "I'm Covered" the energy and passion to speak to thousands of audience members over the past four years.

The song begins with a simple piano introduction that takes us into the opening chorus. This choir sings in a basic three-part gospel harmony with soprano, alto and tenor voice parts, together sending a message of encouragement to listeners about being covered "in the precious blood of the Lamb." The chorus alone serves as a powerful reminder to listeners about our essential need for safety and protection in today's societal chaos. After the chorus is repeated with improvisational support, songstress De-Rance Blaylock leads us into more encouraging words in the verse. After De-Rance's interpretation of the solo, the choir rejoins with the chorus again. De-Rance then takes the audience to a higher spiritual place in the second iteration of the verse which then leads us into the bridge of the song, giving the song more momentum. Following the bridge, there is a declaration from the choir in which they give a big emotional release—which sends strong vibrations into the audience every time exclaiming, "Yes! Thank God, I'm Covered."

The vamp section of this song gives one final cry out to the audience, sharing our thanksgiving for God's covering in our lives every day. This part is followed by a moment of reflection in the song when the choir repeats, "…in the precious blood of the Lamb," until the song concludes with one final exclamation from De-Rance solidifying the power of the message she has so graciously offered us. This song, as a powerful conclusion to the entire production, brings people to their feet every time it is performed.

Thank you, Lord, for giving me "I'm Covered." Thank you, De-Rance, for making my music so special and sharing the message exactly as I envisioned it when writing the song.

I'm Covered

I'm Covered, I'm Covered
I'm Covered, I'm Covered
In the precious blood of the Lamb
In the precious blood of the Lamb

Verse
My God, my rock, in whom I trust.
I take refuge in You,
You are my shield
My Savior, I will call upon the Lord
Who is worthy to be praised,
And He saves me from my enemies!

Bridge
No weapon forged against me shall prosper
When I'm in need, You're always there.
When the storms of life are raging!
When the enemy surrounds me!
My God will cover me,
When I'm in trouble, when I'm lonely
My God will cover me,
Oh, greater is He who is in me,
than he who is in the world!

Vamp
Yes! Thank God, I'm Covered,
I' m Covered,
Thank God, I'm Covered,
I'm covered by His grace,
Covered by His power,
Covered by His faithfulness,
He's been so faithful.
I'm Covered,
Thank God, I'm Covered.

In the precious blood of the Lamb (repeat as desired)

CHAPTER 6

Antigone In Ferguson:
Opening Night Premiere

"The music tells another story that the play doesn't
share. It gives the audience more information and
helps them to understand the story."
~Marcelle Davies-Lashley, alto soloist/choir manager

Thursday, September 1, 2016. With only two weeks left before the performance weekend, the pressure was building. I enlisted the aid of then assistant director of the Crestview Middle School choirs, Melissa Pickens. We spent a few days preparing all the music binders for the *Antigone in Ferguson* choir, stuffing information folders with flyers as well as rehearsal and performance calendars. We collected highlighters, pencils and bottled waters, knowing I had only two rehearsals to make this entire production happen! To be as efficient as possible, I created practice tracks for all the vocal lines in the songs to provide opportunities for my choir members who did not read music to practice their parts independently.

Wednesday, September 14, 2016. I was consumed by a multitude of emotions while walking into rehearsal at the Wellspring Church in Ferguson, Missouri. Still, I was mostly excited to see what would come of this music in which I had invested so many hours over the past month. The first rehearsal was successful; people were excited to start the process and eager to hear the music for the first time. I, too, was filled with joy to hear my music in progress for the first time, and everyone left the first rehearsal feeling encouraged. My joy, however, dwindled, as my mind swirled with the approaching thought that the heart and soul of my music would soon be laid bare to the critique from Bryan in two very short days. Everyone was gracious with me, as I attempted to polish my music to the best of my abilities before dress rehearsal and performance day.

In addition to the music, I also wanted to set the stage for an amazing event. Therefore, I decided to create t-shirts for the choir and team to wear during our premiere weekend. Our music binders and matching uniform pieces for the choir let the team know they were a part of something great. My vision was becoming a reality, and it didn't hit me until our final week of rehearsal that this project was a public presentation made up of my heart and soul. I didn't realize how vulnerable this experience would make me feel, sharing an intimate part of myself with the entire St. Louis community along with an entirely new community of strangers from New York. My efforts to wrap up rehearsals, solve a barrage of problems, book a third performance in a memorable space, connect with choir members and put final touches on the music all led to the moment of truth when Bryan Doerries and his team flew into St. Louis for the final dress rehearsal on Friday, September 16, 2016.

Friday, September 16, 2016. 6:00 PM After a long day at their day jobs, everyone in the choir gathered in the hot sanctuary of the Wellspring Church for our final rehearsal. I was not only sweating from the heat and effort of finishing this music but also from the great anticipation of meeting Bryan. I knew that in a few short minutes I would be receiving feedback from him about the music. During those final moments, I was trying to keep everything running; rehearsals, choir members' needs, soloists' final requests, musicians' needs, last minute copies and seating adjustments, all leading up to the New York team's arrival. The room was bursting with anticipation!

8:00 PM Even though Bryan and his team slipped in the back, we all knew when they had arrived, and I was excited to show him what I had done. When he arrived, I was at the piano finishing some clean up on "Oh Light of the Sun" and not paying attention to what was happening in the dark sanctuary. Suddenly, the choir all started to whisper and discreetly gesture to me to look into the audience—it wasn't very discreet—but I finally glanced to see the long line of people entering the church with Bryan. My heart started racing, unaware that there would be so many people with him; but after finishing "Oh Light of the Sun," I asked the choir to sit down as I went to greet our new friends. I walked to the audience to meet Bryan and a few of his team members and thanked him for the opportunity. I shared that we would perform all of the music and then chat about next steps; he returned his gratitude for my hard work. I formally introduced the choir to Bryan, and then I took the stage for our dress rehearsal presentation of the music of *Antigone in Ferguson*. Due to scheduling, most of the actors were flying in right before our first performances, so this was just a music rehearsal with no actors. The choir and musicians performed all five songs of *Antigone in Ferguson* along with the gospel original I had written, "I'm Covered," in a 30-minute presentation at the end of rehearsal. After we sang this music, I congratulated the choir on their hard work and asked them to go get some good sleep before our debut tomorrow.

I then nervously approached Bryan after giving the choir a few instructions for our big day to finally hear his feedback on our progress toward our premiere performance the following day. Bryan excitedly shook my hand and thanked me for my hard work. Not knowing much about him and his work, I was unsure if it was a pity handshake or if he was truly excited. Regardless, I was relieved that I was able to successfully accomplish, in some form or fashion, something that was acceptable for the performance at hand. During Bryan's remarks before the first performance, I learned that he was truly impressed with the music and my efforts to form a community of singers in the name of *Antigone in Ferguson*. I knew then that I had done something good.

Amongst Bryan's team was Matthias "Teese" Gohl. Teese is a musical genius and close friend of Bryan's; he decided to accompany the team to see what the *Antigone in Ferguson* project was all about. After meeting and talking with Teese, I immediately knew that I had developed a new friendship and mentor. Teese offered to help guide the project musically and add precision and finesse to the production's music scores. After reading his resume and conducting a quick Google™ search, I immediately realized that having Teese's mentorship and guidance was a tremendous honor. Teese has multiple film scores and music-supervision credits with projects, such as *Spiderman the Musical* on Broadway.

9:30 PM I left Wellspring Church after our final dress rehearsal Friday night, inspired and overjoyed at the work my team had done and honored to see this beautiful work shaping so nicely for our big day. With so many thoughts and ideas racing through my head, I didn't sleep much Friday night but couldn't wait to get to the venue Saturday morning to put this all together.

September 17, 2016, 6:30 AM On Saturday morning, I woke up, prayed and got dressed for a day of social justice through the arts. Arriving at Normandy High School around 9:30 AM to set up for our first performance was surreal. I was astounded at all that had been accomplished in such a short amount of time. In talking to Bryan the previous evening, I learned that this process had gained a great deal of national attention. Upon arriving at Normandy High School, I was met with the *PopTech* team from Camden, Maine; the team from *PBS NewsHour*; local news; the team from Athens, Greece and many others from New York.

One part of this project that all of us in St. Louis were excited about was the star-studded acting team assembled for this production. Playing Antigone was Samira Wiley (*Orange is the New Black, The Handmaid's Tale*), the late Reg E. Cathey (*The Wire, Oz, House of Cards*) played Creon, Gloria Ruben (*ER, Mr. Robot*) was Ismene and Eurydice, and Glen Davis (*Jericho, 24*) rounded out the cast as Haemon and the Messenger.

11:00 AM Watching these actors arrive and meeting them for the first time was an honor. What a privilege to have celebrities participate in this experience with *my* music. I was unaware that Bryan had not told the actors that a choir had been assembled for this premiere presentation. Moreover, the choir had not met or rehearsed with the actors. Therefore, upon our arrival, we were all in eager anticipation of what was about to happen. By show time, the choir and the actors were both well-rehearsed in their respective disciplines; therefore, this new experience converged into an exciting feature for the show for everyone, including the audience—win, win! Bryan intentionally didn't mention the involvement of the other participants to allow for an organic collaboration to transpire on stage.

12:30 PM Wow, this was turning into quite a day: I had been interviewed by *Pop Tech* and *PBS NewsHour*, talked to news reporters, warmed up the choir and dressed for our first performance! Duane Foster, fine arts coordinator of the Normandy School Collaborative, was a gracious host. When I arrived at the school that morning, he helped me convert the vice-principal's office into my dressing room, so I had a space to set up all my things and also retreat when I needed a moment of quiet. The best part of my new dressing room was the fan that was providing a little bit of cool air while I was perspiring profusely getting everything ready. Per usual, we were down to the last few minutes before the top of the show, and I was just wrapping up my last interview. I went to check on the choir and make sure that everyone was in good shape.

1:15 PM After I was dressed, I thought of the opportunity that was ahead of me, and I mentally prepared myself to lead these performers through a highly-charged show. I took one final look in the mirror to make sure everything was in place, and then I took a deep breath and headed to the stage—SHOWTIME!

1:40 PM Walking onto the stage for the first time with the actors and the choir was extremely emotional. I had walked onto several stages many times before, but this one was special. Entering the Normandy theater to an audience of a few hundred people with the attentive choir awaiting the downbeat brought my heart joy. The smell of anticipation, as I crossed the black and white checked tiles on the stage, the very stage from which Michael Brown had graduated just two short years prior, settled my anxious spirit. I approached the musicians one last time before we began to thank them for their help. I could not believe that this audience was about to experience music that I had given my all to for the past few weeks and had workshopped with these dedicated singers and musicians for two rehearsals. The choir members all sat eagerly in their seats, as I walked to center stage in my black tuxedo with royal blue accents. We had worked hard and had a full house to perform to—such an exciting moment.

I decided throughout this process I would play lead piano for this production; one, because I wrote the music and would be able to guide the musicians through it more smoothly. Also, directing the choir through the music from the piano gave me the freedom to play missing vocal parts and have a backup in case anything fell apart—I could cover it on the piano. My musicians also played for churches and were very familiar with the gospel pieces sung prior to the show, so I directed those few songs before sitting at the piano to play the show.

1:45 PM The beginning of this project began like the opening to a church service with the singers and musicians gathering and singing together to welcome in the audience and the Holy Spirit. We started with "Total Praise," a gospel standard that would allow those in the audience who were familiar with the song the opportunity to join into this experience, uniting us, right from the beginning. After I walked onto the stage and took my position, the musicians tuned up, the music began and the choir sat attentively waiting for my cue to stand.

Nailed it! "Total Praise" was a huge success! The audience was on their feet enjoying the choir before we had even begun the show— my heart was full. As I was shaping the model for *Antigone in Ferguson,* I thought it best to start with a few familiar gospel pieces to uplift the audience and set the stage for what was to come. All the while, breaking preconceived notions that audience members had when they came into the space. The warm-up music was used as an invocation or invitation of the Holy Spirit, as we would call it in the Black church. This provided a great opportunity for the audience to enter the space and be invited into a mindset to receive the experience *of Antigone in Ferguson* in a way that would open and prepare their hearts.

From my experience programming music, I had thought carefully about what I wanted the choir to sing before the show and the order in which the songs should be sung. I decided the choir would sing "The Blood Still Works" right before Bryan took the stage to welcome everyone into the space, the best decision of this whole process. "The Blood Still Works" was the perfect balance of energy and gospel to invite everyone in the audience to participate in the experience. With over 150 shows under our belt, we have begun every performance with "The Blood Still Works," which has greeted audiences around the world to *Antigone in Ferguson*. The choir, attentive to my every gesture, gave it their all; and after a standing ovation from the gracious audience, we all collapsed into our seats for a short breather before the performance began. I, too, took my seat and found my towel to wipe my brow and took a drink of water before we moved into the main part of the show. I caught eyes with the choir members and then gave them a huge thumbs up; they set a very high standard for the artistic caliber of this production. I was grateful for my choir.

2:07 PM Following the warm-up music, Bryan introduced himself to the audience and explained the process for what we were about to experience in this beautiful celebration of community work in St. Louis. Afterward, we launched into the premiere performance of *Antigone in Ferguson* in the Little Theater at Normandy High School. Experiencing *Antigone in Ferguson* for the first time was life-changing. Hearing the brilliant actors portraying the characters in the story, partnered with the music, created a spirited presentation for the audience. Samira Wiley was captivating; her performance was authentic and genuine. Her level of acting was top-notch and really guided the story for the choir and the audience.

After the actors' opening scene, I had the choir rise to sing the very first song of the show, "Oh Light of the Sun." We went on throughout the performance nailing all of our music! As Reg E. Cathey was giving his final lines as King Creon, the choir prepared to sing "I'm Covered." The song was introduced to the audience as an addition to the show, and De-Rance took the stage to share her interpretation of the song. When we rose to sing "I'm Covered" for the first time, something happened beyond my expectations. I was overwhelmed to witness a room of strangers unite on one accord around this song— regardless of religion, race or place in society. To finish singing "I'm Covered," then turn around to see a room full of tears touched me deeply. I was grateful to be able to sit with such a special song in such a short amount of time and have that much impact on an audience.

The audience was so overcome with emotion that this moment turned into a worship experience for many in the choir as well as several audience members. I looked to Bryan to let him know he could take the stage.

Out of respect for what was happening in the room, he sat back and allowed the Holy Spirit to move in the space. People needed this moment to release a lot of things they had been holding on to—breakthroughs were happening; people were free and open to express themselves authentically. At that moment, I knew that he was respectful of what was happening in the room and acknowledged the power of these lyrics through the amazing vessel of De-Rance Blaylock. It was an indescribably gratifying and emotional experience to participate in this moment with these audience members who were both responding to, and feeling, a powerful experience with something that God had given to me through song. I was completely humbled.

After everyone returned to their seats, a thoughtful conversation began amongst the choir and the audience about the performance and how it impacted our St. Louis community. Bryan returned to the stage, clearly affected emotionally from the performance, and thanked us for the beautiful gift of music that we shared with the audience. Following his brief remarks, he invited four preselected panelists to the stage to take the seats of the actors and share their reaction to the play. One of the panelists was a close friend of Michael Brown, a special moment for all of us to witness and hear his comments. He celebrated his friend Mike and encouraged young Black men to keep striving for excellence, a message that was well-received by the entire audience. It was reassuring to witness panelists who were not celebrities, authors or influencers but rather people from the community.

When all had spoken, Bryan opened up the conversation to the audience. Now just like in any mixed-company situation, many people were reluctant to speak. But once master facilitator Bryan Doerries got the conversation going, to my surprise, we actually had to cut it short, so we could make our next performance that day at another venue. Following the conversation, I decided to bring the choir back for a final song, "I Need You to Survive" by Hezekiah Walker, to leave the audience hopeful for the future of our community.

I did have reservations about Bryan, a White man from Brooklyn, facilitating a discussion with a community of Black people who might likely be triggered from the trauma of the murder of Michael Brown. However, the way he shaped the conversation was brilliant; his gift as a facilitator was obvious during this discussion, as Bryan brilliantly navigated this challenging conversation with our St. Louis community.

After the first performance, everyone was buzzing about what we had built together. My supervisor and long-time friend from COCA, Shawna Flanigan, ran to me immediately with a huge smile, ecstatic over the power of this project. Duane Foster revealed he had not had an experience like that in several years and was thrilled to participate. Still in performance mode, I packed my belongings and prepared to travel to the next venue for our second performance of the day.

As I walked through the now quiet auditorium, since the applause had ended and most had departed, I found myself standing in the auditorium where Michael Brown had spent so much time. My thoughts were reflective on his graduation and past days at Normandy High School. I was instantly catapulted to his nation-shaking death and now to our performance that brought his life front and center. While it is hard to describe all I felt in that moment, there was a resolve, as I left the stage, and yet some indecisiveness about what was to come, as I knew this work was not complete.

4:45 PM When we arrived at Wellspring Church, we were greeted by church members to set up and were excited to see many community organizers and activists with information on their organizations, as we walked in the door. This was really shaping into something great. Still a bit nervous, I took the stage with my team, praying that this audience would find as much value in this project as the first. Interestingly enough during this second performance, there was a distinguished-looking White gentleman who wandered mysteriously in the back hallways of the church, observing the choir's every move.

After becoming increasingly concerned, I asked Bryan if he knew who he was. He smiled and informed me that he was from the Smithsonian Institute and had been with us all weekend, attending the Friday night rehearsal and the first performance at Normandy High School. The *Smithsonian Magazine* was doing a piece on Bryan and including the *Antigone in Ferguson* project in the story. It feels unreal that from day one—*Antigone in Ferguson* has received national attention and has been recognized on many media platforms for its transformative power.

Afternoon and Evening Performances. During the first performance, the actors kept turning around to acknowledge the power of the choir and music, but by performance two and three, it was undeniable the actors were committed and pleased with the new model. During "I'm Covered," they were responding with body language and an outpouring of emotion. In a post-interview, actor Reg E. Cathey said during "I'm Covered" that it sounded like the chorus was saying, "In the precious blood of the *land*," which, in his interpretation, was a powerful takeaway because this gave a broader view to include our nation. Others would later mention this principle, as they transposed this thought to "Purify the City."

I quickly learned the beauty of Bryan's model was that everyone was open to give their own interpretation, and all points of view were acknowledged and received in the discussion. I then realized that I had poured into this music for weeks, and now my job was done. It was now time for the audience to pour out how it had been received. It wasn't about the quarter notes and major thirds anymore; it was about how this music transferred into the souls of others, again another monumental moment in this process for me, as my vision and all my hard work came to fruition.

We had two more impactful conversations after both performances at the Wellspring Church; there were educators talking about the power of this message for students and young people who gave brilliant messages of hope. Similarly, the need for justice came from the elders of the community. Soloist for *Antigone in Ferguson*, Detective John Leggette's mother, Norma Leggette (1934-2017), rose during the conversation to urge all under the sound of her voice to tell the truth. The truth is what is important and will shape how you respond to the future. These words of wisdom from an amazing committee woman who served her community in the 4th Ward in St. Louis, who fought the good fight for civil rights, had a strong impact on the audience.

We performed *Antigone in Ferguson* three times that day to over 1,000 people; and after the third performance at Wellspring Church, I felt a strong sense of accomplishment because I was able to be part of such a powerful act of social justice for our community. During the performances, we experienced emotional breakthroughs from not only audience members but many in our own choir who were hurting because of personal trauma.

Unfortunately, this has become our new normal, as we are faced with deeply distressing and disturbing experiences almost daily from a nation in chaos. We heard a tremendous amount of positive feedback from audience members who said things like:

"I needed this!"

"Thank you for sharing your heart with us."

"I will look at things differently after seeing this presentation."

"My heart is full!"

Comments like these affirmed the vision that Bryan shared with me back in August and provided me assurance that I made the right decision to join this amazing team. After a long conversation reflecting on our weekend experience with a few of the choir members, I drove home and mentally prepared to go back to my life as a middle school music teacher—not knowing that this was only the beginning of *Antigone in Ferguson*!

Returning to my students at Crestview was such a joy, as I had been splitting my time to get this project on its feet. They were excited to hear about its success, and we jumped back into music preparation for our concert in a month. I was so excited to take a breath and get back into a routine with my students. I apologized to them for the crazy first two weeks and shared the amazing opportunity to write and perform music for over 1,000 people and share the stage with brilliant stars such as Reg E. Cathey, Samira Wiley, Glen Davis and Gloria

Ruben. Flabbergasted by the cast, they immediately started googling me to see how big of a celebrity I was. I smiled and told them I was not a celebrity—kids are hilarious! I ended up receiving praise from the administration and even a shout-out from the superintendent.

Getting back to normal felt really good. I was able to start planning lessons for my kids, prep music for our first performance and try to get into a groove with my students. It was important to me as the choir teacher to spend many hours with my students building relationships and finding what worked best for each of my music scholars. All students learn differently, and I recognized and respected that in my classroom; and with such large classes, it took time to connect with each one. Therefore, an active effort was necessary to build rapport. Within a few days of getting back to school, I had filed away the music and the *Antigone in Ferguson* experience as a great short chapter of my life. But things would change drastically yet again with a single phone call.

A few days later, I received another phone call from Bryan indicating that the foundation who hosted the project in St. Louis wanted to bring us to New York to perform in the lobby of the Onassis Center. I dropped the phone in shock. After regaining my composure, I delineated all the details for the event in an email to my choir, the Phil Woodmore Singers, inviting them to New York to perform the *Antigone in Ferguson* project, sponsored by the Onassis Foundation USA.

Event planning is one of my strengths, so before our first New York performance, I set to work preparing my team for this new collaboration. I learned in a phone call with Bryan that we would be working with a production team called THE OFFICE, who produced many projects around the world and were collaborating with a local New York choir led by an amazing NYC artist named Marcelle Davies-Lashley. So many unknown factors, so many loose ends—how would I make this work? I spent the next several days in shock but trying, yet again, to maintain order in my classroom while planning another experience of a lifetime for myself, the Phil Woodmore Singers and my new team members.

The new challenge in this situation was not a 30-day music writing period but teaching a group of strangers my music across the country. After several calls with Marcelle, she was excited to collaborate, and I swiftly sent her the practice tracks I had created for my choir and then planned a few more St. Louis rehearsals with my music team as well. To everyone's surprise, the trip to New York was fully funded, and we received stipends for our time. As we approached the performance weekend in October, just a few short weeks after our premiere in St. Louis, my anxiety crept back up on me. But I prayed, packed my bag and left for the airport for my next *Antigone in Ferguson* adventure.

CHAPTER 7
From Ferguson To Greece

"I am a strong believer that the audience knows more than the performers, and we [the production staff and cast] are here to learn from the audience."
~Bryan Doerries, director

We arrived in New York in the fall of 2016 to perform at the Onassis Cultural Center. Bryan shared that we would be partnering with Marcelle Davies-Lashley and her choir, Voices of Hope. I was so excited! Marcelle is an accomplished performer and music leader in New York City with over 25 years of experience in the industry. She and her group greeted us warmly upon arrival, and we immediately formed a bond that broke many barriers. In performance, especially vocal music, there is real value in artists being well-acquainted and having trust on stage.

I sat everyone in a circle for introductions. When it was Marcelle's turn, she announced, "My name is Marcelle, and I hate the police!" She described how abusive police officers were in New York City and how they grossly mistreated people of color. I was proud that my team of law enforcement officers did not become defensive. They, in turn, introduced themselves and their positions in the St. Louis Metropolitan Police Department. They talked with Marcelle and acknowledged her position, that we would soon find out was shared by many of our audience members. They reassured her that not all law enforcement officers were corrupt.

One special bond Marcelle made was with my good friend, Captain Latricia Allen. Captain Allen is a natural-born comedian. She spent time making Marcelle and others laugh, putting all at ease, and the dialogue helped to create space for vulnerability in the group. The process of getting acquainted with each other was a needful time that greatly enriched our rehearsal time together, as we no longer felt like strangers, but professional singers and musicians working together to prepare for our New York City premiere performance.

Marcelle and her team brought an added layer of talent and skill to the team. She really put my mind at ease when she assured me that she had my back, much needed in our new unknown stomping ground of New York City. All in all, after meeting Marcelle, I felt good returning to the hotel and still couldn't believe I was in New York about to premiere my musical work, just a few weeks after the St. Louis premiere.

Waking up in New York City on performance day, I was excited and motivated to swiftly knock out my to-do list, so I could have a little fun. After pulling together some loose ends, I went over to the performance space on 5th Avenue to get ready for our dress rehearsal. We knew the space was not a traditional theater, but I walked in to find a dark, plain office lobby that I was not sure we could transform into a theater space.

Upon entering, the crew was setting up the stage for *Antigone in Ferguson*. I was doubtful that this dark office building lobby with a stale aesthetic would serve as an adequate space for the performance, but I immediately set to work to provide a quality experience for my choir and the audience awaiting our performance. Our dressing rooms were upstairs in the office suites of the Onassis Foundation. After sound checking in the lobby, meeting our acting team and making sure all things were in order, I went up to get dressed for my New York premiere.

My heart was flooded with emotions—why were such good things happening to me? How did I go from a classroom teacher to a music composer and conductor with a New York premiere so quickly? After getting dressed, I went to the lobby of the office suite to greet the rest of the choir who were all in great anticipation. I gathered the choir and musicians, shared some encouraging words and then we all traveled down the elevator to enter the performance space. I paused as I got off the elevator and was honored to find the hundreds of seats filled in the lobby with a standing-room-only crowd of people huddled around the seats waiting to hear my music. I had to fight my way through the mob of eager audience members to make my way to the piano for the pre-show music.

Everyone hastily got to their places, the musicians began playing and the choir began to captivate the audience with the inviting warm-up songs; it was happening! As we moved further into the warm-up music, the audience began engaging with the choir, and the magic of the transformative power of music started to happen. I kept pondering over the same question, "Would these New Yorkers be just as excited about my music as the St. Louis community?" We ended with "The Blood Still Works." The choir sat with a sense of pride and accomplishment, as the audience applauded us with great vigor and enthusiasm. Bryan came to the stage to set the scene and introduced our four actors, and the show of *Antigone in Ferguson*, premiering in New York City, was underway. The opening scene between Antigone and Ismene was flawless. I cued the drummer, turned and had the choir stand, smiled at them, as we all took our unifying breath, and so we began our rich, melodious and serious compositions!

Hearing my music in this space was a truly powerful experience; I was so humbled to have the support of our New York choir friends who sang my music with complete enthusiasm. I caught glimpses of the audience as the choir was singing, and their body language and emotions reflected satisfaction; it appeared that everyone was enjoying the project.

When it was time for "I'm Covered," I took the stage to introduce the song and set the scene for the audience. This was the first time I had really seen the audience from this vantage point; my eyes misted over with joy and jubilance after thinking of this opportunity and all that transpired in the past 48 hours. I finished my remarks, and De-Rance took the stage. I didn't get to see the audience's reaction to "I'm Covered" but felt we had done something great when I turned from the piano and the choir to a standing ovation from the audience before we even sang the final phrase. Again, not a dry eye in the house, "I'm Covered" was a real impactful moment in this show, and the amazing De-Rance Blaylock was the right choice to lead the way during this moment in the performance.

"We just had church in the lobby of the Onassis Center building," one of the participants shared with me afterward. We transformed this corporate lobby into a sanctuary of high praise. "I'm

Covered" seemed to have an external trigger that reached the depth of the soul with this audience, like a mighty wave of love, hope and peace; everyone seemed to be sincerely moved in this space. The highlight of the entire weekend occurred when Marcelle sat on the panel and shared the story of how she declared that she hated police in front of all these amazing officers from St. Louis. She proceeded to tearfully embrace her new soul sister and friend, Captain Latricia, with whom she had formed an immediate bond during this process.

The newly formed relationships were evidence of the power of this project and how this show brought people together in a very special way. *Antigone in Ferguson* brought an open and loving spirit upon the audiences that allowed for honest conversation and a change in thinking to happen. After experiencing this unprecedented performance, I knew this was going to be a life-changing production and collaboration!

Following the Onassis Center performance, I returned to St. Louis inspired and ready to continue teaching at Crestview; when, surprisingly, I was graced with more good news via my email. Just a few days later, we were invited to perform at the *PopTech* Conference in Camden, Maine, where we shared a portion of the *Antigone in Ferguson* music and facilitated a conversation with conference attendees about the project's importance to our present-day society. The momentum continued with a return to St. Louis for a performance at COCA and on to Baltimore in January 2017 for a performance at Coppin State University, for nearly a thousand people.

Then I received a call with some unbelievable news. Bryan stated that *Antigone in Ferguson* was invited to perform at the Stavros Niarchos Foundation [16] Conference in Athens, Greece, that same summer. Awestruck, I exclaimed, "What?!" The band, the Phil Woodmore Singers and I were invited as guests to perform at the Summer Nostos Festival with a public performance for the people of Athens, all expenses paid.

---

[16] https://www.snf.org/ (Stavros Niarchos Foundation Website)

After several months of planning, I traveled with my entire team to Athens, Greece, in the summer of 2017 to perform our first international show, less than a year after its inception. By this point in the process, the St. Louis music team was in awe of the amazing opportunities this project had afforded them and was honored to be participating. De-Andrea Blaylock-Johnson, now the assistant director of the Phil Woodmore Singers, shared with the team during one rehearsal that a few choir members were anxious about details for an upcoming performance. However, she encouraged everyone to calm down and just wait for me to email the details. She began calling the emails, "Magic emails from Phil."

Returning from New York and being asked to participate in a few trips throughout the year was shocking to the choir and me, but when I announced the opportunity to go to Greece, other singers and musicians in the community quickly began asking me if there were any free spots in my choir or band.

Now that the stakes were much higher, I yet again set out to prepare and organize my music team for this new challenge. I updated the score with Teese Gohl and created detailed music rehearsals to tighten up the music for our international premiere.

Arriving in Greece, I was ready to put on the performance of a lifetime. We were fortunate for the chance to conduct a week-long workshop of the show, giving us time to digest the music in a new creative space and make necessary changes to the flow of the show and music halfway around the world. The Stavros Niarchos Foundation was so gracious; they treated us like celebrities—I didn't know what to do with myself. My mom and dad flew ahead of me to Greece with the Phil Woodmore Singers. While at the front desk of the hotel lobby, my mom noticed that a limousine had arrived. The front desk staff began to chatter among themselves, "Is that him? Is that him? Yes, that's him; let's go greet him."

My mom became interested in who was garnering so much attention, so she started moving with the hotel staff towards the door. Hoping it might be Kenny G, her favorite saxophonist, she too would get an autograph. And then, having taken a flight from a different destination, I stepped out of the limo! She says her mouth literally dropped open in shock. She responded like I was a celebrity with goosebumps and became very misty-eyed. She waited to let me have my moment before greeting me. Mom said she then returned to her room to sit and stare at the wall, taking in what had just happened. I was completely unaware of this until much later when she shared this scene while taping my upcoming documentary, and she became misty-eyed again. I think we all felt like celebrities our first time in Athens!

One of the most powerful moments of the trip was an impromptu conversation that happened between the law enforcement officers who were on the trip and a few of the civilian choir members. After a year of performing, the civilian choir members were now ready to start opening up about their true feelings about law enforcement and how they had been affected by police officers in their lives. The conversation became really intense and emotional for some, but it became quite revealing for the choir members to talk about the "breakthroughs" that occurred in this interaction. The transformative work was now affecting the choir on a very organic level and was providing a platform for this level of deep conversation amongst the chorus. Another amazing moment during this trip involved my brilliant father, Pastor Willie Woodmore, the guitarist in the band. Upon arrival in Athens, we were notified that Reg E. Cathey was unavailable to play Creon which meant David Patrick Kelly needed to step in. With this last-minute change, Bryan wanted my father to portray the role of Tiresias which involved a dramatic reading oh his lines. I chuckled, "Why not?"

My father left his place in the band and went to the actor's position to get set up for his scene. As he began to orate the lines of the monologue, everyone turned around in awe at his brilliant acting skills. One of the collaborators asked where he went to acting school, and I responded with a humorous comment simply in jest!

My father had not taken an acting class ever in his life nor had he had any interest in theater or ever participated in any theatrical productions prior to *Antigone in Ferguson*. He was with this group primarily to support me and the work that I had done.

These two stories and many other experiences will always live in my heart from my time in Greece. Meeting the incredibly talented

Anika Noni Rose, who played the role of Antigone, and David Patrick Kelly, who played the role of Creon, along with the other excellent performers, was the opportunity of a lifetime.

After many memorable experiences and rehearsals during our workshop week in Greece, it was time for our dress rehearsal and sound check in the performance space. I will never forget the feeling of walking into that capacious opera house and looking out into all of those 1,400 empty seats. I have performed on many stages in my career, but nothing like this. Our show and dialogue were over-the-top, enhanced by our perfect surroundings. We bowed to an audience that was clapping and standing. I felt so happy and thankful to all the people that helped make this moment happen. We went backstage to celebrate. Looking heavenward, I gave the largest and longest sigh of relief. Suddenly we heard the loudest noise—was that applause? Indeed, it was! I peered through the curtains to another standing ovation!

In an instant, Bryan appeared and said the audience wanted us back for an encore! Even though some had scattered, I was determined to give the audience what they wanted. We took center stage again with joyous faces and performed a final song to another standing ovation! The Athens Opera House was in thunderous applause again. We bowed, yet again! Every whistle, shout and clap were resonating within me. All unnecessary apprehension I had experienced had turned into intense excitement and happiness. My adrenaline took me places I did not think possible. I felt invincible; like I could compose and conduct with the best of them. What a musical rush of confidence. The Greek people had welcomed my music. My first time in Greece—I loved the people and the experience of their culture. I was even more thankful for the support of The Stavros Niarchos Foundation. Their home felt like home.

After two powerful performances for the people of Greece, we were proud of our work and accomplishments during our time there. Some of the greatest minds in the world gathered at The Stavros Niarchos Foundation international annual conference, but the most special performance was for the people of Greece when we were able to open our doors to the local people and get their feedback on how

Americans reenact Greek tragedy. Even though we didn't understand what the Grecian people said about our performance, the roaring, ongoing applause and the audience's request for an encore proved that my music resonated as a universal language and spoke to the hearts of countless people in another culture in the greatest of human experiences. My very being leapt for joy! We also were blessed to witness the flawless performance of my father, Tiresias, energetically delivered for the Grecian people; and after receiving a huge applause after his scene, there was no turning back. Pastor Willie Woodmore had officially been cast as Tiresias. My father would go on to play Tiresias in both runs in New York and at many performances around the country, even becoming recognized for his phenomenal portrayal of Tiresias in a stellar review by Ben Brantley in the *New York Times*.

What a surreal experience to witness my musical work onstage in a beautiful Opera House overseas at a Greek festival. In just under a year, *Antigone in Ferguson* had gone from a conceptual wild hunch to an internationally acclaimed project. I returned to St. Louis after Greece to finish vocal directing a production of *Beauty and the Beast* at COCA, before heading to Brooklyn for the next portion of our *Antigone in Ferguson* adventure. In July of 2017, we had the privilege of performing for the community of Brownsville on a basketball court for over 1,000 people, not including people watching from their apartments and the rooftops of surrounding buildings.

The back-and-forth of intermittent summer performances and returning to school in the fall had become my new way of life. After Brownsville, our production team was preparing an impressive college tour for the 2017-2018 season, traveling to Dartmouth College in Hanover, New Hampshire; Williams College in Williamstown, Massachusetts; The College of the Holy Cross in Worcester, Massachusetts; and the Historically Black College and University (HBCU), Harris Stowe State University in St. Louis, Missouri. In February of 2018, the Brooklyn Public Library joined as our partner and invited *Antigone in Ferguson* to come perform at the library in a series of performances. We also had the opportunity to present *Antigone in Ferguson* during the 50th anniversary weekend of Dr. King's speech, "The Drum Major Instinct," at the New York Public Library on

February 3, 2018. The duration of consecutive performance runs never lasted more than two or three shows: we would arrive in a city, prepare the show, perform and then return home. It was a wonderful experience and exhausting, but I was honored to be sharing this important work with so many different communities across the country.

Following the tour, the Rockwood School District showed me a grand gesture of support by granting me a second sabbatical (which had never been given before in the district) to aid me in conquering musical efforts in the world of New York City. During this sabbatical, I was able to put on a five-week run of *Antigone in Ferguson* in the Off-Broadway theater, the Harlem Stage, and invest time and energy meeting with producers and agents and building a voice studio in New York.

CHAPTER 8
The Structure of *Antigone In Ferguson*

Antigone in Ferguson had a large impact on my perception of my own race. After going through the show, I realized a bias I had about my own race. I followed society in categorizing the image of the Black man. I placed a cause behind police shootings rather than actually believing that White police officers were shooting based off of their own bias.
~Terrol Stone, chorus member

From the numerous performances, trial and error, different models with the choir and research from my dissertation, we have created a fluid model for *Antigone in Ferguson* that allows audiences to be involved at a highly-efficient level of engagement and receive a plethora of takeaways. From the moment the audience walks in the door, they are enveloped in an immersive experience.

To ensure diverse participation, Theater of War Productions provided different audience members with transportation to the production and offered light refreshments before the show. These groups, from places such as senior citizen homes, church groups, youth-in-crisis programs, not-for-profit groups and other marginalized communities in NYC, were given preferential seating and treated as very important person (VIP) guests. TOWP believes those with firsthand experiences in injustice, classism, racism and the many issues facing society today are the real VIPs, not just those with privilege or a long list of credentials who may be out-of-touch with the reality of others' experiences. Organizations and VIP guests are acknowledged at the top of the show during opening remarks from Bryan and the co-facilitator.

As part of the pre-show environment, a slide show reveals the lives of choir members through photographs, videos and interviews. This first element draws the audience to the chorus members before the performance even begins. This is important because it provides the audience with a glimpse of the lives of the chorus members outside of the show and portrays their humanity, making them more relatable.

This is not fully conveyed through the production, and the slideshow helps the audience understand that most chorus members had other professions and lives outside of music, while yet the sound, stage presence and power of the chorus might make them believe otherwise. Furthermore, this element helps to express the creative team's desire to form a democratic body of singers in the production. The audience learns from the slideshow that the choir members included law enforcement, educators, social workers, activists, a sex therapist, Ferguson residents and government workers among others representing various backgrounds. This diverse body of singers comes together to present this project in a unified effort, with the intent to have an audience of strangers unified as well during the performance and discussion.

Twenty minutes prior to the opening scene, while the slideshow presentation is running, the chorus and musicians present three songs to sing as warm-up music. This music has been included to set the mood for this immersive experience since *Antigone in Ferguson* premiered in St. Louis. This opening music experience is reminiscent of worship service in churches pastored by Black ministers. The songs have been familiar to audience members in Christian communities as well as audience members who strongly connect with Black culture. However, we've had many members in the audience who are not religious, unfamiliar with the selected songs and who have never heard gospel music, still enjoy the music immensely.

The key is in the way I teach expression when teaching the music to my choir members. Whether it is my personal composition or a gospel anthem from Richard Smallwood (such as "Anthem of Praise") or traditional gospel from James Cleveland (such as "God Is"), when I drill down (teach) every note into the depths of my choir members' souls and work to relate the text to real-life situations, they develop the ability to pour these notes out (sing) in such a melodious format, that whether audience members are familiar with the music or not, the music experientially resonates deeply within their souls. As we have heard time and time again, this euphoric response was the first time for many. The feeling of well-being is therapeutic in an emotionally healing way, and this new attitude carries them into the performance.

Even though there are many spiritual elements of this production, Bryan invites all feedback and views through different lenses as a part of this discussion. Therefore, members of the faith community can connect with this spiritual expression as well as people with other religious or non-religious beliefs and backgrounds.

Following the warm-up music, the artistic director and co-facilitator emerge to greet the audience and share about the experience in which they are about to take part; then the show begins immediately with the opening scene between Antigone and Ismene. The production itself elicits frequent interaction between the chorus and the actors (characters) in the show. The confluence of the chorus and the performers provides for a cohesive storytelling model that speaks in powerful ways to the audience, as is traditional in Greek theater. The chorus acts as the psyche and the voice of spectators (both as participants in the play and audience members) because they reveal opposing viewpoints and opinions.

The show is about an hour and fifteen minutes long, concluding with the dramatic gospel power ballad, "I'm Covered"—a pinnacle moment in the show that encourages heartfelt conversations about social justice. A large part of the performance process for Bryan and Theater of War Productions is about authenticity; therefore, throughout the entire production, the fourth wall is broken on multiple occasions, sometimes intentionally and sometimes as a matter of impulse or improvisatory expression. Following the performance, the facilitators, including Bryan, appear to begin the post-show discussions with four panelists. The four are representatives of the community and are introduced—not as celebrities or politicians—who stand in front of the audience to initiate the dialogue and model a way forward. Next, the facilitators step out into the audience to solicit audience members' responses, asking three or four guiding questions for about an hour. Bryan reminds the audience that the discussion is the most important part of the event, as it places audience members in the position of experts on their own life experiences and ultimately amplifies their voices. Following the post-show discussion, the chorus returns for a final departure song. I selected a song that helped usher the audience into a heartfelt position of gratitude and peace—a song that would carry them from our space and back into the real world. Oddly enough, it helped to recognize that whatever we were going through, it could always be worse. It also helped when we reflected upon our personal portion in life and were thankful. Peace and contentment were ours when we gave thanks for what we had been spared from and even what we were going through, especially when we believed in the divine power that took us through it all.

Therefore, I selected "Thank You," written by Walter Hawkins (1949-2010) that addresses various tragedies that come under the umbrella of God's divine grace, mercy, love, power and protection. For every show, we brought the actors back in, and they actually sang this last number with us. Some of the actors were a bit more nervous about singing over acting, and many commented that this was their first time performing in a choir, though they really appreciated the model. Some were in disbelief of what they had experienced. We ended every performance with "Thank You" to a standing ovation audience.

After our last song was over, the intensity and color of the stage lighting was turned off, and the general lighting for illumination was turned on. All of a sudden, it was like recess time with my kiddos in middle school. Everyone was lively and full of excitement. They talked with people who sat around them; they rushed the stage to meet the actors, choir members and me. We shook hands, gave hugs, took pictures and exchanged business cards. Finally, the time arrived to move from the main performance area to the lobby, for our long-awaited light refreshments. We heard often there were thoughts and salivation for the cookies that Bryan mentioned at the very beginning of the show. With every performance, we provided the most wonderful tasting cookies—normally sugar and chocolate chip. That was an exciting time for all, including the choir members. Detective Leggette called it our "milk and cookie time." I appreciated having the extended time after the show to linger for great post-show conversations in such a low-key way.

De-Andrea Blaylock-Johnson, De-Rance's sister and my former colleague from Melody of Praise Gospel Ensemble, is one of the zestful facilitators for the post-show discussion of *Antigone in Ferguson*. De-Andrea and I worked together for five years leading the Melody of Praise Gospel Ensemble, St. Louis University's gospel choir organization. Ten years following our college experience, we had the opportunity to reconnect during a concert series, which I was asked to participate in at Fee Fee Baptist Church. When we needed a spokesperson for the group at a performance, I asked De-Andrea to represent the group, and Bryan was so pleased with her thoughtful comments that he asked her to come on as a facilitator for many other performances of *Antigone in Ferguson* and a later collaboration, *The Drum Major Instinct*. De-Andrea became Bryan's co-facilitator after many performances, including the Harlem and Brooklyn runs of the production. De-Andrea has contributed a wealth of knowledge and insight to the post-show discussion and has supported the production with her talents and skills in therapy and local activism in St. Louis, Missouri.

Since the show's inception, I have observed chorus members, actors, audience members, staff, ushers and all involved, be transformed by the experience that *Antigone in Ferguson* manifests through this innovative model. We worked collectively to create a safe space for a conversation to happen in an enlightening way during rehearsals and performances. Our desire was for the audience of strangers to become like the chorus, speaking out about the plot, it's collective actions and central themes, bravely in one safe space. Our powerful conversation allows for diverse perspectives which enable audiences around the world the ability to hear different perceptions on current relative topics.

That aspect of the model is based on the incredible work of Augusto Boal when he made the audience members the actors, calling them "spect-actors" in his book, *Theater of the Oppressed*[17]. As Bryan Doerries states, "The show is an experience, not a performance." The audiences are key participants in the show, as much as the actors and singers on the stage. Each night, we begin the show in great anticipation of what

---

[17] Boal, A. (1985) Theater of the Oppressed by Augusto Boal New York: Theater Communications Group, 1985.

the outcome will be during the discussion. For anyone who has experienced the warmth of the Black church, we see this as a traditional welcome from the hosts inviting guests to "kickback, relax, open your mind and hearts to receive and feel like you are at home." With this in mind, audiences interpreted Byran's comments in different ways and responded differently to the show because of this fact. The spect-actors in *Antigone in Ferguson* are given full permission to respond from their hearts to the experience of *Antigone in Ferguson.*

CHAPTER 9

Antigone In Ferguson
Premieres Off-Broadway

"Never underestimate the wisdom of the chorus during a tragedy, onstage or in life. It is the gospel chorus reacting to confrontations among the characters that viscerally lifts [*Antigone in Ferguson*] into timelessness. Conducted by Phil Woodmore, who also composed the music, this choir includes social workers, law officers and teachers from St. Louis and its environs, among other places. In other words, they know what they're singing about. Lushly blended in layered harmony with detours into virtuosic solos, their voices swell in wonder, praise and sorrow at the mysteries of life and fate."

~Ben Brantley's review of *Antigone in Ferguson* in the *New York Times*[18]

Countless planning meetings, conversations and emails surrounded the process of arranging the first five-week run of *Antigone in Ferguson* in the fall of 2018 in New York City. We were tremendously blessed to receive a grant from the Stavros Niarchos Foundation to fund the entire production and to ensure that it would be free to the public. As a testament to the community of Ferguson and the roots of the project, I proposed bringing a portion of the original choir to take part in the seven-week process—two weeks of rehearsals and a five-week performance run. The original budget allowed for eleven of the St. Louis singers and musicians to participate in the seven-week process, and then I was able to hire ten additional singers from the New York City community to perform with the St. Louis core group.

This was a challenging task because I still wanted a democratic body of singers like the St. Louis premiere choir. Therefore, before my arrival in New York, we put out a notice to a few audition blogs and

---

[18]https://www.nytimes.com/2018/09/14/theater/antigone-in-ferguson-michael-brown.html

75

emails to several networks to advertise the audition. We also asked a few local artists to send the information out to their community networks. Through these connections, we sent information to the New York City Police Department (NYPD), local churches and a few social justice groups.

After many conversations with venues in New York, we finalized a contractual agreement with Harlem Stage. As stated on their website, "Harlem Stage is a performing arts center that bridges Harlem's cultural legacy to contemporary artists of color." The Harlem Stage Gatehouse has been a New York City landmark building since 1890 when it was built as the pivotal facility within the Croton Aqueduct Water Supply system. This building was restored in 2006 into a flexible performance and rehearsal space. What was originally a source for distributing fresh water to the city is now a vital fountain of creativity, ideas and culture. With its rich history, the creative team knew the Harlem Stage[19] was a very appropriate space for the show.

I arrived in New York in August of 2018 to set up for this life-changing opportunity. Upon arrival in NYC, I had a few days to settle in my new apartment (two blocks from the Apollo Theater). I was ecstatic to have these accommodations and be able to reside in the heart of Harlem for a few months. I was within walking distance of the theater as well, so I was able to commute by foot, which allowed for much easier travel arrangements during rehearsals and meetings.

After getting settled and adjusting to my new environment, I held three days of auditions for the New York core singers. Forty-five singers auditioned; twenty were called back. I was able to offer contracts to ten people. Two of our sopranos were professional vocalists in the NYC area while another soprano had been auditioning frequently and was working at the Lincoln Center. One of our altos was a well-known musical force in the New York community, leading choirs and performing all over the city. Another was a professional singer in New York, and the third alto was a college student who took a semester off school to be a part of the New York production. One of the tenors was a New York police officer, and another was a

---

[19] Harlem Stage: https://www.harlemstage.org/

newcomer to New York from St. Louis. One of the basses[20] was a choir director in the area and an outstanding pianist. The other bass was a student from Columbia University in Chicago who auditioned for the show and agreed to take a semester off to be a part of the production. These musicians comprised the diverse body of singers who joined our St. Louis choir members, and they became the "core" choir who were contracted and sang each performance at the Harlem Stage.

As a part of the rehearsal process, and in support of the model created by Theater of War Productions, I began this rehearsal with a focus group of the thirteen choir members we cast from New York for the Harlem Stage run. This allowed me to become better acquainted with the singers from the onset and also gathered everyone together to share our individual views on topics being explored throughout this process. Initiating a candid conversation during the rehearsal process helped to buffer the difficult conversations that the choir would sit through each night.

Beginning with a conversation on our first day truly enabled the choir to launch into this model in a productive way and also gave them permission throughout the rehearsals to make personal connections with their colleagues, even outside of the organized conversation. This was a generative conversation, and choir members found many similarities amongst themselves during this focus group. I also learned a lot about the choir members and the experiences from their past that brought them to audition and eventually be chosen to be a part of this production.

I have used this model of vulnerable conversation all over the country when putting together new singers for my projects. One specific conversation I had during this time will stick with me forever. In a four-hour rehearsal session before a performance at an arts conference for the state of Virginia, I brought together a group of singers from a local church. This was a very willing group when we began the conversation. It was beautiful to hear from one of the elders of the group who shared about his traumatic experiences of racism

---

[20] Refer to the Glossary for further information on the term *bass*

growing up in the 50s and 60s, especially in the South. Then the youngest member of the group shared a chilling story about being pulled over and having his car ransacked by a police officer with no explanation and no warrant. Everyone in the room paused, breathless, after he shared that he was, "Thankful he made it home alive," realizing the gravity of that statement in today's world.

The diversity of age and sharing in this group was important to the process of the show and the best way to build community within the choir. This, in turn, trickled down to the audience during performances. During the conversation, there was one gentleman named James McClure who didn't like speaking publicly and indicated that he didn't have much to share as I began the exercise. I was emphatic in my opening remarks before that in this group conversation; everyone was given the freedom to share as little or as much as they wanted to during our time. This was a safe place where everyone was supported and appreciated for their point of view.

After hearing a few candid conversations from members in the circle, James McClure, a young man seeking a career opportunity in Los Angeles (L.A.), shared a story about being attacked by a Special Weapons and Tactics (SWAT) team in his home due to racial profiling. He began by telling us that he moved to L.A. with a close friend, who was an aspiring black female film composer. She needed a roommate, and the L.A. Opera Company was being formed by opera legend, Placido Domingo, so he thought it would be a great way to get acclimated with the company by planning to audition for the opera chorus. James gave a firsthand account of those traumatic events that happened to him in L.A.:

> I moved from North Carolina two days prior, and I was renting a home from a college professor. We specifically asked her to tell all her neighbors we were Black and did not want trouble, and we belonged there. It was my second day in Pasadena, California. I was getting settled in my place, and I got myself locked out. So, I went in through the back door to get back in the house. I was literally in pajamas. I went back in the

house to continue my job searching when I thought I heard a noise. I looked out of the window, and several police officers were out there. One yelled through a megaphone, "If you are in the house, you need to come out now!" I was so confused, so I walked outside, hands up. At this point, I was trembling. They threw me down on the ground with my face in the dirt. They cuffed me and held me down on the ground. I was humiliated.

They were about to put me in the car when I asked, "Is anyone going to ask if I live here?"

One officer replied, "You live here?"

I answered, "Yes, I moved here from North Carolina two days ago."

He replied sarcastically, "Welcome to L.A."

They kept me for 20 more minutes, searching the house and asking me about different items to make sure I actually lived there. At this point, I sat on the ground, shell shocked and trembling.

One cop looked at me, and he whispered in my ear, "If I were you, I would not move."

It was the most chilling and sobering thing. It just came over me. I could have lost my life! That was the first time I really felt that it is dangerous to be a big Black man living in America.

This is an all too common occurrence for people of color in the United States and is a distressing encounter this young man would never forget. I shared my shock, frustration and empathy for this young man and thanked him for sharing his story with us. As I was listening to the story, my heart was troubled because this very much sounded like domestic terrorism against a person of color.

It is also just a fraction of the long history of terrorist tactics used by governmental and law officials in the United States, targeting Black and Brown Americans, dating back to the slave patrols and the formation of the Ku Klux Klan (KKK). Some police raids like these are really for the same purpose: to use violence to control through fear, intimidation and harm. The excessive use of force he experienced will be trauma that will live with him for the rest of his life. Petrifying moments like these are the reason this work with *Antigone in Ferguson* and other social justice projects are so important. I will never forget hearing this story and will carry it with me when I put together focus groups in the future. After the focus group and rehearsal in Richmond, we had a stellar performance for the art community of the state of Virginia. I was happy to make these new connections and friends.

Returning to the focus group for the Harlem Stage run, after our conversation, I had a rehearsal with the choir to begin learning the music from the show, including the pre-show music. Through these thoughtful discussions as a group of singers (but more importantly a group of human beings), they started to make strong connections to core values and beliefs to lead us forward in solidarity through this process. After this intense week of music learning and important dialogue, we had a week off in which I made edits to my evolving score and updated parts of the *Antigone in Ferguson* process.

Following our break, eleven people from the St. Louis premiere choir arrived to represent the original cast of the St. Louis version of *Antigone in Ferguson*, for the entire five-week run in Harlem. We proceeded with another round of rehearsals to blend the New York core ensemble with the St. Louis group to form the new *Antigone in Ferguson* singers for the Harlem Stage run. The St. Louis choir members were able to make personal and musical connections with the NYC choir in ways that I would not have been able to accomplish on my own without my team.

During the planning phase of each production or show run, a creative team member from THE OFFICE collaborated with me to find a community choir or group to participate in each week of the production during a run. Therefore, for the five-week run, we located five community-based choirs (community or church choirs) to participate in this process. After a few weeks of planning and preparation, with help of our producing partners at THE OFFICE

Performing Arts + Film[21], I secured five different organizations: United Voices of Hope, R.Evolución Latina Choir, First AME Church Choir, Riverside Church Inspirational Choir, and Bethel Gospel Assembly Church Choir. Once these choirs were identified and agreed to work with us, choir leaders worked with their individual choirs on the music of *Antigone in Ferguson* as well as the five gospel pieces that were the invocation prior to the production. Each week of the run at the Harlem Stage, a different community choir performed with the core choir. This allowed for a new energy each week.

We then invited all the community-based choirs to participate in a Community Music Day. At this event, I invited the *Antigone in Ferguson* core choir to join with all the new singers to model the various nuances of the music. This provided an opportunity for all participants, not only to sing together, but also to hold a brief conversation about the specific elements of this process that are unique to Theater of War Productions' events, especially regarding *Antigone in Ferguson*. This was another opportunity to demonstrate the transformative power of music and the use of music as a platform for vigorous conversation. Furthermore, this was an informal opportunity for the core choir to share with the additional community singers the structure and process of *Antigone in Ferguson*, while being receptive listeners and ambassadors of the project. This provided an outlet for the community-based choir to share personal stories or emotions that may have arisen during brief discussions on the Community Day or the singing of the music during rehearsals.

During the Community Day rehearsal, we met many people who had a passion for music but also had a passion for activism. One young man thanked the team for offering this opportunity because he did not know how to process his cousin being killed by law enforcement, and this was a needed outlet for him. It was refreshing to meet so many in the community who had the same values and mission as the *Antigone in Ferguson* team. In addition, we met those who were uncertain of our mission and process and needed more

---

[21]THE OFFICE: https://www.theofficearts.com/

information from the staff. This was our opportunity for a teaching moment. There was a young lady from one of the church choirs that did not understand why so much "church music" was intertwined with the show. Explaining some of my inspirational journey in my music writing satisfied her concern. Overall, just sharing the good news of *Antigone in Ferguson* with the people who had some misunderstandings made it worth the time and effort to hold this event. It was amazing to see all the emotional breakthroughs even in the rehearsal phase of the show.

One young lady's grandmother had passed away a year earlier. She shared while we were singing "Total Praise", that she had the most vivid memory of her grandmother and was suddenly brought into a place of comfort and relief. "Total Praise" was her grandmother's favorite song. Many questioned the use of police officers in this project, including a young man who had lost a family member to police brutality. This allowed my team to help the unsure participants understand our intentions and furthermore, allow the police officers to offer a different perspective in a safe space. Hearing from the young people who were highly motivated during this process musically and in their activism filled my emotional tank; I was overjoyed to see the amount of people who were ready to tackle these issues and problems in the communities we were performing in during the show run.

The "open house," that included all the participating choirs under one roof at the same time, was exactly what the singers needed. It was hands-on, experiential teaching. It was evident that day our message needed to be heard. It was decided that many of the community choir members would attend a performance to hear either their favorite choir or to be more informed about the expectations of them when their week arrived. This process was also hands-on for me with the huge task of sharing this show with thousands and adding a new team to our existing team every week. Teese Gohl was skeptical of the change in the model, but I had confidence and was determined to pull it off. After our soul-singing, we had soul food. What a great Saturday Community Day rehearsal kickoff for *Antigone in Ferguson*!

After our Community Day rehearsal, we went into an intensive tech week[22], bringing in a different community choir each night of tech to experience the show in real time, and also provide them more context about the show structure before the actual performances. Also, during tech week, the crew adjusted the sound for the space, including striking a balance between the band and choir, along with any lighting adjustments and blocking needed for specific choir members throughout the performance.

Following four tech days, we performed two dress rehearsals, the second being an invited dress rehearsal for special guests of the production team. Then, we put on a preview performance for the media. I woke up on Preview Day, of all days, extremely ill and knew that I would not be able to participate in my most-anticipated performance. Unfortunately, I did not have a substitute for this production, and a very loose contingency plan was created if I wasn't able to function. Bryan called me and asked how bad I felt. I told him I felt very bad; but if I could walk, I would be there. I took a long hot shower and got dressed in an effort to make myself better, but the illness persisted. It took every ounce of energy that I had to make it into the venue.

Once I arrived, people told me I looked pale. I sat in the dressing room, virtually lifeless, while everything was being organized. I came onto stage for the warm-up music and was only able to stand to direct the first song before I had to sit at the piano bench and just play. The bright lights and blaring sounds triggered a strong migraine, and I just felt too physically weak to continue sitting up all together. After the choir sang "I'm Covered," I gathered my belongings, caught an Uber™ back to my apartment and collapsed on the couch for the rest of the night. I prayed and willed myself to feel better for opening night but was still really sick during that performance as well. Finally, by the third performance of the show, I felt better and able to participate in the full process—pre-show and performance, discussion and closing number. After struggling through the first week of

---

22 Refer to the Glossary for further information on the term *tech week*

outstanding performances of *Antigone in Ferguson* from the newly formed *Antigone in Ferguson* Core Choir and Voices of Hope Choir, I was feeling much better; and by week two, I had fully recovered.

We presented four more weeks of sold-out performances for thousands of people from Harlem and the surrounding communities of New York. The beauty of performing this show Off-Broadway was that this venue provides for an extremely diverse audience of people who live in and visit New York to enjoy our production every night. It was incredible to hear the many stories of audience members who were inspired by this production and felt compelled to share their stories. These testimonies were an important part of this process, as people of different faiths, races, backgrounds and beliefs came together to find a way forward in unity. Theater of War Productions had never conducted an extended run of any of their productions before *Antigone in Ferguson* in Harlem, and the tremendous success of this run created a great deal of buzz in the New York City community for weeks following our 30 performances.

After the experience of the five-week run of *Antigone in Ferguson*, I returned to St. Louis to continue working in music education, teaching voice lessons, collaborating with COCA and beginning analysis on the data collected for my dissertation. Then, I started working on my next show with Theater of War Productions, *Frederick Douglass in Staten Island*, a chamber piece I created around a speech that Frederick Douglass presented to the National Convention of Colored Men in Louisville, Kentucky, on September 24, 1883. I created music to accompany the speech that was presented by eight performers rather than the large choirs of *Antigone in Ferguson*. There was an abundance of potential plans for *Antigone in Ferguson* and other projects after I returned to St. Louis for the winter, but the final decision was made to produce a ten-week run of *Antigone in Ferguson* in the spring of 2018 in Brooklyn, New York. One of the limitations of performing in smaller confined spaces was the inability to openly invite all people to enjoy our production each performance. Therefore, we found a larger space, a church in a centralized area: St. Ann and the Holy Trinity Episcopal Church off of Montague Street in Brooklyn, New York.

This church was in an iconic area in Brooklyn, a block from the famous Brooklyn Bridge that spans the East River and connected us to Manhattan! This popular and hopping area of town provided many shops, restaurants and other attractions for the community. But more importantly, this church was in such a populated area that during showtime, people would hear the music and wander in to see what was going on. "The doors of the church were opened," and many people stopped by to be a part of this incredible experience.

Our time in Brooklyn was very rewarding. Working through several issues, such as how to cool the church down during the heat of summer and cram 50 singers on a stage set for 40, also made things interesting; but through it all, we had a successful and transformative run in Brooklyn. On the final night, my mother pulled Bryan aside and asked him if she could have the final word. She had been reading Michael Brown's mother's book, *Tell the Truth & Shame the Devil, The Life, Legacy, and Love of My Son Michael Brown*, and wanted to bring Mike's words into the room before we ended this process.

After sitting silently through almost 100 shows, Alma Woodmore, First Lady of *Antigone in Ferguson*, stood on the last night, the 50th production at the church, to read some of Michael Brown's last Facebook posts to a standing-room-only audience of well over 800 people. She needed to share Michael's Facebook post that was included in Lezley McSpadden-Head's book. Michael had posted just 12 hours before he was murdered. There was one specific post that touched my mom's heart and brought her to her knees in tears:

August 8, 2014, 3:22 AM
"I could use a hug right now FR" [for real]

My mom wept, as she realized that this child was reaching out for a loving touch—not to be murdered. It is easy to say, "I cried because it could have been my son." But she cried that night because it was Michael Brown, and he was a human being. How dare the laws be written in a way to justify such a senseless murder.

Mike's mom had been at our production the previous evening and Mike's dad, Michael Brown (Big Mike), had been with us on opening night at the Harlem Stage. My mom was hard-pressed that the last night in Brooklyn needed to be Mike's night—she felt the urgent need to bring his humanity into the space—she knew this was apropos. As it would be, the audience agreed with applause.

~Rest in Power, Michael~
The cast and crew of *Antigone in Ferguson*
love and miss you

CHAPTER 10
Antigone In Ferguson Transforms Lives

Antigone in Ferguson very deliberately tackles themes that people struggle to openly talk about today. Most importantly, it leaves people feeling first, and thinking second—and I think all art serves to provoke thought and feeling.
~Jonathan Elkins, chorus member

Antigone *in Ferguson* is a unique concept which allows its audiences, participants, staff and cast to experience a transforming piece of art that has the power to change the world. Through the sensitive topics of the story of Antigone, partnered with the beauty and vitality of the music, *Antigone in Ferguson* pierces the heart in ways that other performances cannot. The following are some of the captivating perceptions that audience, cast and crew members contributed during the after-show discussions.

Since its inception, *Antigone in Ferguson* has been a valuable resource for struggling communities and marginalized people, providing them with a voice in discussions surrounding civil unrest due to systemic inequalities in policing (profiling, harassment, brutality, killing), criminal justice (higher incarceration, longer sentencing), education (under-resourced schools, more severe discipline, over-representation in special education/underrepresented in gifted programs), healthcare (lack of access and affordability), housing (unhealthy living conditions), financial/economic opportunities (low home ownership, wages) and employment (discrimination). These, along with other issues, prevail in marginalized communities all over the country and many situations are left unaddressed. All of these tactics are intentional to maintain unequal social status and lack of social mobility for many Black and Brown citizens. Through the work of Theater of War Productions, the creative team has created a specific model that makes a space in which many moving parts work simultaneously to create this artistic expression and experience for audiences across the country, as well as to provide a place to spark a much-needed dialogue for many traumatic experiences.

Following the 2016-2018 national tour, I was inspired to change the research topic for my dissertation from the changing voice of middle schoolers to the transformative power of music through the experience of the auditioned choir members from the fall 2018 run of *Antigone in Ferguson* at the Gatehouse Harlem Stage. For the basis of this research, I used Mary L. Cohen's Theory of Transformation which she applied to her work with prison choirs. The theory states that there are complex relationships through the sung texts, the choir's social and cultural contexts and interactions with audience members that enhanced inmates' self-perceptions and afforded them the potential for positive transformational change.

During my research study, I drew upon topics that paralleled those in the theory: complex relationships through the sung texts, choir's social and cultural contexts, interactions with audience members and choir members' enhanced self-perception through the process pertaining to social justice issues. In applying this theory to the members of the *Antigone in Ferguson* choir, my intent was to use the same model of socializing, goal-setting and discussing life outside of the choir, to build a case that the theory of transformation has provided a platform for the participants to be transformed through the show's music. I collected the stories of seven chorus members from this production to create a narrative about their journey through the process from beginning to end. This research was informative and groundbreaking, as I documented firsthand how the music I composed for the show inspired and transformed the lives of these seven individuals in such an organic way.

As a part of my dissertation research, I also conducted an extensive review of the literature on homeless choirs, intergenerational choirs and prison choirs. From this literature review, I created a rehearsal and show model that allowed me to meet with participants of the chorus, band and production staff to have an open dialogue with and amongst themselves in this process. The transformative power of music provides a positive platform for the musicians and singers in the show to express themselves through the music and to protest social justice inequities in our present society. Many people shared with me and others in the *Antigone in Ferguson* staff that they were honored to participate in something that was so meaningful and allowed them to express themselves so strongly in an artistic way. Furthermore, there seemed to be a spirit of anticipation in sharing difficult issues in a safe space that gave them the courage to be open and honest. I completed my research and dissertation work in the spring of 2020 and graduated with a doctorate in music education, with emphasis in choral conducting and voice pedagogy, in May of 2020.

After trying many formats for starting this rehearsal process over the past four years, based on my analysis of the focus group, I concluded that beginning with an open conversation with the chorus members contributed to the success of *Antigone in Ferguson*. Another key element was to allow time throughout the process to discuss the elements of the music (texture[23], pitches[24], dynamics[25], lyrics and mood) and to be able to process any feelings the show might evoke. In addition to the hour and fifteen-minute focus group, I made sure I checked in multiple times with the chorus members (formal and informal) to continue the conversation throughout the rehearsal process. These discussions served as a template that enabled them to informally continue conversations during breaks before and after rehearsal, allowing for a deeper connection between the chorus members and a feeling of safety, as they navigated portions of conversations that might be more sensitive or problematic.

I believe everyone who attended the focus group interview was open and honest in this setting and felt empowered to share their opinions with the group. It is always important to remember that in life, as with musical performance, people will not always agree but need to find a way to cooperate and cohabitate. The experience of *Antigone in Ferguson* allows people to come together to discuss sensitive issues that could generate new ideas and hopefully, solutions to the problems discussed. Through this conversation, many people in the chorus felt encouraged that we took the time and effort to become better acquainted through this process, starting with an understanding of

---

[23] Refer to the Glossary for further information on the term *texture*
[24] Refer to the Glossary for further information on the term *pitches*
[25] Refer to the Glossary for further information on the term *dynamics*

each other's stories. As the musical composer and director, it was important for me to know the initial perspective of each chorus member, as it helped me gauge if anything was effective for the research. Teaching music is only a part of what is needed to be successful for this experience. Transformation happens when chorus members are engaged in a musical process that is meaningful to their lives on a deeper level that's more than just music.

When dealing with matters that are potentially emotionally charged, it is necessary for the facilitator to be educated on the matters at hand and fully prepared to manage these challenging conversations. While each discussion and process of this magnitude is unique to the set of participants, this structure can serve as a guide for productive ways to manage dialogue centered on these topics. During my experience, the use of relationship-building activities also provided for a productive music rehearsal process which appeared to contribute to the positive experiences of the chorus members.

The most rewarding aspect of serving as the director was having the opportunity to spend ample time, collectively and individually, with chorus members. During these moments, I was able to obtain an informal baseline on many chorus members' personal ideologies on issues, as we started the process, and then see how those changed over the course of this production. The most striking story of transformation from my research came from the leader of the Voices of Hope Choir, Marcelle Davies-Lashley, who stood in the initial focus group and declared, "I hate police!" Since one of the philosophies of Theater of War Productions is that everyone is allowed space to express their opinion, no one in the room lashed out at her when she made that comment. She was able to share at the conclusion of this project that she now loved her new police officer family and hated "bad police officers," not all law enforcement. This was a powerful moment for everyone in the room, as she shared how this process had transformed her thinking.

During my rehearsal-break conversations, many performers shared private testimonies with me about how they had been dealing with a variety of issues. We were working on the song "Thank You," which closed the production every night, and a chorus member pulled me aside and expressed they had recently been struggling with finding purpose in their life, and rehearsing this song gave them the motivation and hope to persist. Another evening, one singer approached me and divulged that before this project they were homeless and didn't have any hope for living. However, after rehearsing this music and being amongst such positivity in this process, they found a new outlook on life and were excited for their future. Another impactful evening for all of us occurred when one chorus member shared how much they struggled with suicidal thoughts and didn't see a purpose in living. They had dealt with this challenge prior to participating in this production but felt inspired to share with us that suicide is a "real thing and people deal with it every day."

The impact of this process and the show seemed to be endless: one participant shared that this production completely changed her way of thinking about social justice and White people; another spoke on the transformation they saw over time from relating the play to their experience as a mentor, and another observed the impact made on the audience. These stories were significant parts of this process for me and for other chorus members, as they shared with one another. One participant shared in a personal conversation with me that the music spoke to her soul in such a way that created courage in her to speak publicly, which she did not possess prior to this process. These are just a few of the many examples from this production that have shown me the exceptional significance of this work that helped many to reconnect spiritually or emotionally to bring about hope, peace and even joy to live and fight the good fight another day, unlike they had experienced before.

There are also countless stories of transformation in the audience every night, and I have chosen a few of those moments to share later in this chapter. The music of *Antigone in Ferguson* also invited new and different audience members who connected strongly to music but might not otherwise attend theatrical productions. Many stood during our post-performance conversations and stated that this was their first theater experience, yet they shared insightful comments about how the show affected them and gave them insight on a multitude of serious topics, such as hatred, suicide and depression.

Many stories shared in the experience of *Antigone in Ferguson* supported the notion that music can be transformative and have a lasting effect on members of the choir as well as the audiences.

Below are a few quotes from their interviews and our dialogue during the project that I felt articulate the transformative power of music in this communal healing environment. During the run of the show at the Harlem Stage, many choir members commented on how this show enabled them to feel things deeply embedded in their psyches. Below is a reflection from a choir member at the end of that run:

> I witnessed the power of art and saw its impact on many ideologies that filled the room each night. I think most, if not all people, left with a new way of thinking about a bias that they may have.
> ~Terrol Stone, chorus member

The beauty of this process was that the choir participants were given the same level of conversation within the choir as intended for the audience. The next quote from a NYPD officer gives some perspective on policing from an officer's point-of-view—one who is striving to remain upstanding and serve his community with integrity:

> As a police officer, it is hard to wear so many different hats in life: police, pastor, father, community member; and I hope that this process will help everyone to see that I am not just a police officer—I do so much more.
> ~Sergeant Marcus Lewis, chorus member

This next quote from a younger choir member sheds light on how impactful this project is on awakening audiences to the issues that need to be addressed:

Before *Antigone in Ferguson,* I would have said we were lost as a society and helpless, but now I think there is a little bit of hope. Doing programs like this and meeting other young activists give me hope for our future. Seeing older people who want to listen and encourage our younger generation also gives me hope!
~Carolynn Clyne, swing soloist[26]

I love the next quote about the transformative power of the arts. It was reassuring for me to hear about this transformation from a choir member which was confirmation for the labor of love I sacrificed to complete this project on time. I am a firm believer that the arts are transformative. The arts are powerful. The arts do change people's lives. The arts bring communities together. The arts heal. The arts save lives. The arts supplement and provide a missing component that is necessary for growth in all humanity:

It is my firm belief that the arts are transformative, and someone could be seeing their first or last show in the audience. It is important to always tell the story. I hope the audiences connect with us. I know we can tell this story to so many people. One of my main hopes is that this performance can spark an important conversation that needs to happen within our community.
~Jonathan Elkins, chorus member

As a researcher, composer and music director, it was important that I minimize my personal bias out of the process. Therefore, I kept a journal throughout the rehearsal process and run of the show to record our successes and challenges and also my thoughts and reactions to different moments in the process that I wanted to remember.

---

[26] Refer to the Glossary for further information on the term *swing soloist*

We all benefited significantly to work with individuals whose strength and resilience were exemplary. Many traveled to New York as integral parts of our production, including post-show panelists. From my journal, the following poignant moments stand out from the course of the 10-week run at the St. Ann and Holy Trinity Episcopal Church in Brooklyn, New York:

Journal Entry 1: One evening, the choir and actors delivered a beautiful performance, leaving the audience in awe of the production. The four panelists for that evening took their seats in front of the audience of 1000 members to speak about their reactions to the performance. The final panelist to speak was a middle-aged White man who shared how he really enjoyed the show and connected mostly with the amazing music. He was a guitarist and used to work at a music store. He gave a few other pieces of information from his life experience and then divulged that he and his wife were the parents of one of the children who was killed in the Sandy Hook mass shooting. When he shared this, the room went completely still. Then, three seconds later, the audience and creative team slowly stood to their feet and gave him and his wife a standing ovation.

Watching events such as Sandy Hook on television saddens my heart, much like when then, President Barack Obama, openly wept over the children of the Sandy Hook massacre on national television. To shake the hand of a man who lost a child in this tragedy was a totally different experience. The realness of that encounter will stick with me for the rest of my life, and many in the audience commented on how striking it was to meet this couple. Beyond his presence, it was so inspiring to hear his story and the actions he and his wife are taking now to impact change in our society and to honor their son.

Journal Entry 2: Another impactful moment was the evening that Gwen Carr, mother of Eric Garner, who died because of aggravated strangulation while in police custody in New York, attended the show and sat on our panel. She spoke about the need for love, respect and unity in the midst of adversity in today's society. When she took the microphone and introduced herself, again, a stillness fell over the room, followed immediately by a standing ovation from the entire audience and the *Antigone in Ferguson* staff. Many mothers in the room became very emotional, thinking of all that this mother has endured trying to find a way forward after the police murdered her son. It was such a beautiful testimony to observe her tenacity, courage and grace in such a terrible situation. In her book, *This Stops Today,* Mrs. Carr quotes Reverend Al Sharpton, activist and founder of National Action Network, "There are two sides to every story. I believe the policeman has a side. I believe the victim has a side; but there is only one truth." Mrs. Carr titled her book *This Stops Today* because these were some of the last words Eric Garner, her son, spoke to the police officers who took his life using a banned chokehold. It was an example to this audience of how one finds strength in adversity and builds a positive platform from tragedy and a terrible situation. She is an example for many mothers around the nation whose children have been murdered while in police custody.

Journal Entry 3: Gwen Carr was so impacted by our production, she decided to return to see the show again with 30 of her closest friends, whom she calls "The Mothers of the Movement"[27]. "The Mothers of the Movement" are mothers of young men and women of color who have been murdered by police officers or gun violence. This social justice organization was started in 2013 after George Zimmerman, who fatally shot Trayvon Martin, was found not guilty of murder. In Trayvon's parents' book, *Rest in Power, The Enduring Life of Trayvon Martin, A Parents' Story of Love, Injustice, and the Birth of a Movement*, they raise awareness to the impact of gun violence and racial profiling on families of color.

Lezley McSpadden-Head, Michael Brown's mother, "Rainbow of Mothers"[28], was in the audience with "The Mothers of the Movement." In her book, *Tell the Truth & Shame the Devil*, Mrs. Head shares in the "Introduction, My Truth," Mike Mike, as his family

---

[27]https://time.com/4423920/dnc-mothers-movement-speakers/ (Information on Mothers of the Movement)

[28] http://michaelodbrown.org/index.php/rainbow-of-mothers/ (Michael O.D. Brown We Love Our Sons & Daughters Foundation

lovingly called him, had only his daddy's first and last name. His full name was Michael Orlandus Darrion Brown. Michael Brown's parents had given him his own identity. Therefore, he is not Michael Brown, Jr., as the world mistakenly calls him.

This moment became full circle for me. Meeting Michael's mother created a level of reality for me and the audience that didn't exist when speaking about the horrific events we saw over and over on television. To hug a mother who had loved and lost her son, to listen to a mother weeping while sharing her story and to hear a mother crying out, as she expressed her unrelenting deep hurt, will forever reside within my soul.

The inexpressible dissatisfaction with what is happening in our bleeding nation brings an awareness of how incomprehensible these tragedies are and a new level of compassionate understanding to me, and hopefully others, with listening hearts about the essentiality of *Antigone in Ferguson.* The arts in general have not only given voice to this conversation, but also, they are a beginning to the healing process that is so desperately needed in our nation. We weep as we pray for *just mercy.*

These three moments are an infinitesimal portion of the striking experiences beheld by the *Antigone in Ferguson* creative team during our post-show discussions. Another powerful moment for us was when Michael Brown's father, Michael Brown, came to one of our first shows in Harlem. Listening to Mr. Brown talk about his son, in the context of the show, was heart-wrenching. Following meeting Mr. Brown in Harlem, he invited The Phil Woodmore Singers to participate with his organization, "Chosen for Change[29]," at the fifth anniversary of Michael's death. During our performances, we heard from people who felt emotionally better because of the music, people who were deeply moved by the dialogue and interaction with audience members, people who questioned their beliefs and the beliefs of others, youth who gave profound rhetoric that changed the adults' way

---

[29] https://www.facebook.com/MichaelBrownFoundationCFC/

of thinking and finally, we heard from many of our elders who imparted priceless needed wisdom.

One evening after an *Antigone in Ferguson* performance during the run in Brooklyn, an older Black woman, wearing a hat that said "Spiritual Gangster," raised her hand to speak multiple times and was finally called upon to give the final word for the evening. This passionate and loving woman stood and said she was in her late nineties and was honored to be amongst the land of the living. After receiving a standing ovation, she spoke truth to the audience in a wise way—sharing that she loved life and having good days, she went on to share that she had outlived all of the undertakers whom she was paying to bury her. After stealing our hearts and the show, she got up and danced with one of the choir members during the final chorus— unforgettable. This was the prevailing psyche that took over the room after many *Antigone in Ferguson* performances

CHAPTER 11
The Art of Discussion

"In fact, when we try to talk openly and honestly about race, White fragility quickly emerges, as we are so often met with silence, defensiveness, argumentation, certitude and other forms of push back. These are not natural responses; they are social forces that prevent us from attaining the racial knowledge we need to engage more productively, and they function powerfully to hold the racial hierarchy in place."
~Robin J. DiAngelo, *White Fragility:*
Why It's So Hard for White People to Talk about Racism

The quote above from Robin DiAngelo, regarding White fragility and how challenging it is for some members of the White community to talk candidly about racial issues, social justice and inequalities in marginalized communities, became a reality during my experience with Theater of War Productions post-show discussions. I witnessed many people show their avid support of marginalized communities, not to mention the sentiments expressed of wanting to see change in our political system. However, there were people who spoke during the discussion who had strong oppositional opinions.

As stated earlier in this book, one of Bryan Doerries's main missions is to create a safe space for all people to share their truths after his shows. I witnessed the power of this exercise during many performances over the many years we have performed this show. However, with all of the stories of transformation, healing, discovery and support that came from several of these conversations, all things were not positive. The beauty of this process and this show is that the platform, which is formed for the audience from experiencing this show, is that your gut reaction, unfiltered thoughts and unedited questions are the best comments offered during the discussion. Many people revealed that they had to overcome apprehension and even fear of giving their opinion before they spoke publicly. On the other hand, some people were quite confident and comfortable sharing their views (even if they were controversial).

Everyone is entitled to their own opinion, and the only way we can move forward is to air out the opinions of the outliers and allow their voices to be heard in order to help begin the process of awareness to all in the audience.

Even though many of our after-show conversations were brief and pleasant, some could be very lengthy and intense. Many people during the audience discussion wanted to talk politically. At the Harlem Stage, one Black lady said her niece surprised her, and she did not know what she was attending. If she had known, she would not have come because she was tired of hearing about Ferguson on the TV. It was all too heartbreaking. Then she said, "Everybody is talking about Creon and how he is the epitome of Trump. Well, Creon has a lot of ways like me—so I need to change!" This was a profound moment for this audience member and an inspiring moment for the audience because she gave everyone permission to think within themselves about things that need to be addressed in all of us.

Several striking moments also happened during our run at the Harlem Stage. Not everyone who spoke after the show had completed a positive transformation. One evening, there was a woman who rose to speak of her disgust with the production and not being able to get past why police officers were performing on stage about Michael Brown. We learned later in the evening that she was a frontline protester during the riots in Ferguson, Missouri, and was struggling with post-traumatic stress disorder (PTSD) because of those days and nights on the Ferguson frontlines. During a post-show discussion with the young woman's family, her brother shared his hope that this show would help his sister begin to heal from her trauma of being pepper sprayed by the police officers, but unfortunately, her needs were beyond the exercise of the show, at least in the immediate aftermath.

There were people during the post-show conversation and after the show who had expressed that they stopped attending church; yet the *Antigone in Ferguson* experience had given them the liberty to go back to church. Many had been away from the church for years for various reasons—judgmental attitudes and hypocrisy. On a different night, there was uncontrollable laughter, when one lawyer said, "Since I feel like I've been to church this week, I don't have to go this Sunday;

I can stay home and watch football!" Each night was an emotional rollercoaster from heartfelt tearjerkers to sidesplitting anecdotes. It was all needed, and it was all good!

During a presentation at a university on the East Coast, a lively group of thinkers were ready to respond to the production without the need for guided conversation from Bryan. We heard comments like:

~I am pleased with my White privilege and do not see the need to change.

~I am a Black woman and have been passing as a White woman.

~I will not apologize for my White privilege.

~I am transferring to another school because of unresolved race problems here.

~I do not like that the White Creon laughs at the Black Tiresias's advice.

~I now feel free to share for the first time in my life that I am a lesbian.

There was even a young White college student who said, "When Black men get angry, they are really scary. Tiresias, the blind prophet, scares me. I am just scared by angry Black men." Of course, my initial reaction was to jump to my dad's defense, who played Tiresias in this production, but leaning on the open model Bryan had created and giving everyone space to share their opinions, I let her comments sit in the room and let the conversation develop organically. There were many interesting things shared during this college visit. During this performance, I learned that some in higher education have a different world view on other communities. Moreover, I saw the radical views of professors being challenged by the progressive views of many students in the audience as well. There were many honest things shared in the discussion that night—having an opportunity to speak openly in this setting appeared to be a strong help to many in that college community.

The aforementioned highlights from our discussions are a small snapshot of the hours of conversations that were had with audiences all around the world. We were honored in August of 2020 to celebrate the sixth anniversary of Michael Brown's death with a virtual presentation of *Antigone in Ferguson* over Zoom™ (because of the COVID-19 pandemic) with performances from actors live from their homes and five of the soloists live from their homes as well, singing along with pre-recorded tracks of the music. Matt Craig, sound engineer extraordinaire, developed an application that was able to control the Zoom sound system and allow multiple singers to perform live over the platform without the latency issues that arise on Zoom meeting calls when multiple people are trying to speak at the same time. During this virtual premiere, 48 countries were represented during this presentation and almost 7,000 people tuned in to witness this groundbreaking work. Again, a thoughtful and inspiring conversation ensued following this virtual presentation, proving the power of this project can be felt through the internet and in people's homes.

As we continue to adapt to the growing differences of this "new normal" life during the pandemic, the Theater of War Productions staff has worked to create dynamic virtual presentations to continue their work across the country and world. We have scheduled several opportunities to witness a virtual presentation of *Antigone in Ferguson* during the fall of 2020. We hope to collaborate with different universities in 2021 in similar models, as gathering restrictions are lifted. Even a pandemic can't stop the "Antigone in Ferguson movement."

The *transformative power of music* is not a coined term by music educators, but a living and breathing entity that allows birth, growth and progress in people's lives. I saw this transformation firsthand in my research with the *Antigone in Ferguson* choir members. They shared the most profound statements about how this production has done much to change their way of thinking, shifted their mindset and helped them to grow in ways they didn't know possible.

I also have been transformed by this project. Writing this music, much like writing this book, was a true labor of love that I offer to my community as an artistic gift. My love, passion and creative intelligence were breathed into these lyrics and the music. However, my transformational experience didn't occur until I heard and witnessed my music on stage in context of the entire show for the first time. Transformation happened in me the day when I realized that my contribution to activism in my community was through this artistic piece—activism through the arts! Finally, the unreal experience of witnessing all of the audience members who found solace in the music and comfort in the experience was captivating and life-changing in and of itself. Music is a powerful medium that creates a space for everyone to speak their truths.

CHAPTER 12
Final Thoughts:
Where Do We Go from Here?

"And may we never forget what happened here,
and never go to war again…"
~"Oh Light of the Sun" lyrics from *Antigone in Ferguson*

According to an article in the *Washington Post* about the use of lethal force by police officers since 2015, Black Americans were overrepresented among all those killed by police under all circumstances[30]. This disturbing truth has proven itself over and over in many communities across the United States and has left many families broken and looking for answers. The underlying themes of the play are Antigone's conflict between society's need for proper law and order and an individual's need to follow their conscience or what is true and right, as well as the "psychological devastation that comes in the wake of a social disaster."[31] The result of social disasters can be psychological wreckage that is enormous and the scarring of the collective psyche[32]. Stage Director, Timothy Moore, explained in an article about a version of *Antigone* he brought to St. Louis following Michael Brown's death, that Greek tragedy in performance can respond to contemporary events in remarkably powerful ways. The intermingling of ancient drama and modern politics, however, often bring controversy. The songs of *Antigone in Ferguson* reflect the controversial subject matter and can be categorized in the genre of protest music (or music for social activism) because the themes in this play elicit critical dialogue around social justice.

This concept in the history of music dates back to the beginning of the civil rights movement, a profound time for music in

---

[30] Beer, T. (2018). Killings of Blacks: Data for 2015, 2016, 2017, and first half of 2018. The Society Pages. Retrieved February 15, 2019, from https://thesocietypages.org/toolbox/police-killing-of-blacks/

[31] Moore, T. (2016). Sophocles after Ferguson: Antigone in St. Louis, 2014. *Didaskalia*, 13(10), 49-68.

[32] Weinert-Kendt, R. (2014, October 10). Upstream Theater's 'Antigone' neither avoids nor exploits #Ferguson Echoes. *American Theater Previews*.

United States history. In a review of literature for my dissertation, I found that there has been a great deal of discussion concerning the civil rights movement and the ways in which it deconstructed and reconstructed democracy, citizenship and education[33]. In my dissertation, I shared that the modern civil rights movement emerged in the South, where a protest tradition was and remains firmly rooted. The movement broke from the protest traditions of the past in two ways. First, it was a time where Black citizens organized en masse to directly confront and effectively change the deeply embedded systemic inequalities among groups and institutions responsible for their oppression[34].

Secondly, this was the first time in American history that Blacks adopted nonviolent tactics to bring about social change. Music played an important role in this nonviolent protest movement. Civil rights music, or protest music, became a uniting force, giving voice, empowerment and amplification to silenced voices. Many artists have used the performing arts as a means of activism for years. Famous artists have been sharing the story of the Black experience in America through film, literature, music and dance by people such as Ava DuVernay, Spike Lee, Toni Morrison, Nina Simone, Katherine Dunham, and Alvin Ailey, to name a few of my favorites. The work of these incredible artists of color is a part of the collective body of contributions to the arts and serves as a conduit for social change.

Social activism through the arts has had a strong presence during most of African American history, dating back to slavery and the use of spirituals and code songs, as a tool to communicate and cope with the atrocities slaves endured. In an article written about the great work of Dr. Martin Luther King, Jr., Anthony Trecek-King describes how many of the pillar musical moments in U.S. history are related to social justice. For example, jazz and blues were birthed from the Jim Crow era, and the art form held emancipatory themes of politics, race

---

[33] Rabaka, R. (2016). *Civil rights music: The soundtracks of the Civil Rights Movement.* Lexington Books.

[34] Woodmore, P (2020). *Antigone in Ferguson: The experience of Seven Members of the Democratic Chorus in a Social Justice Musical Production.* [Doctoral Dissertation: University of Missouri-Columbia]

and culture. Jazz artists of the 1960s such as Art Blakey, John Coltrane, Charles Mingus and Max Roach, to name a few, became politically active. Duke Ellington and Dizzy Gillespie, for example, played several benefit concerts for civil rights organizations.

Trecek-King argued that jazz was a symbol of social progress. He discussed a composition Duke Ellington wrote in the summer of 1963 entitled, "My People," which was based on the cultural contribution of African Americans and was meant to be used as a tool to educate adults and youth about Negro history[35].

Protest through the form of music has since carried over from the 60s, and many other artists have used music as a platform to protest, such as Sam Cooke ("A Change is Gonna Come" [1965]), Otis Redding and Aretha Franklin ("Respect" [1967]), James Brown ("Say It Loud-I'm Black and I'm Proud" [1968]), Curtis Mayfield ("We're a Winner"[1968]), Nina Simone ("Mississippi Goddam" [1964] & "Young Gifted and Black" [1958]), Public Enemy ("Fight the Power" [1988]), Lenny Kravitz ("We Want Peace" [2004]) and more recently Alicia Keys ("Perfect Way to Die" [2020]). And as pop star, Beyonce Knowles-Carter quoted, "It's been said that racism is so American that when we protest racism, some assume we are protesting America."

Also in my research, I gathered information on social justice and the role that music played during the civil rights movement. Rosenthal and Flacks explained in their book, *Playing for Change*[36], that most Americans are aware of the freedom songs of the 1950s, 1960s and 1970s associated with the civil rights movement. The Reverend Jesse Jackson once noted that, "While mass action—marches, sit-ins, boycotts and the like—created the body of [protests during] the civil rights movement between 1955 and 1965, 'the music breathed its soul'."

In this instance, and many others during the civil rights movement, music was used to uplift and bring encouragement to marginalized communities. Mahalia Jackson, Aretha Franklin, Sam

---

[35] Trecek-King, A. (2016). On our way: Programming a Martin Luther King, Jr. concert for youth choir. *The Choral Journal, 56*(8), 10-21.
[36] Rosenthal, R., & Flacks, R. (2015). *Playing for change: Music and musicians in the service of social movements.* Routledge.

Cooke, James Brown, Nina Simone and other acclaimed musicians and artists of the civil rights movement gave me a framework from which to compose the music for *Antigone in Ferguson* with its goal to advocate for positive change in society. Rosenthal explained that songs, singing and singers are an integral part of changing the world.[37] A message through music can shake the foundations of an established order.

Music as a form of activism has become a profound tool in affecting change during many pivotal times and places in history and around the world. Music can serve as a vital element in compelling a community to not only accept diversity but to value and embrace its unique contribution to society. The music of *Antigone in Ferguson* is modern-day protest music, and its highly successful use demonstrates that music has the power to stimulate critical dialogue in communities to strive toward social justice.

The more recent stories are still too many: the Satilla Shores neighborhood in Brunswick, Georgia, where Ahmaud Arbery was jogging one morning in February of 2020, and was murdered because a White father and son duo said they saw him as a threat. Or George Floyd, who allegedly told Minneapolis police officers that he couldn't breathe while being suffocated to death from three officers on top of his body while one looked on, as a video would alert and alarm the world. And Breonna Taylor, shot to death in her own home after police used a "no-knock" warrant to invade her space while she slept after her shift as a healthcare worker. People of color are frequently being racially profiled, which leads to the involvement of police officers for fraudulent reasons in public places and even minor traffic offenses, that result in killing an innocent person. Often, many years later when the statute of limitations prevents prosecution for these crimes, the truth is told. In many of these cases, the truth is told as a deathbed confession or to clear one's conscience, not out of consideration for the human life lost.

---

[37] Rosenthal, R. (2001) Serving the movement: The role(s) of music. *Popular Music and Society*, 25:3-4, 11-24, DOI: 10.1080/03007760108591797

This was the case with Emmett Till's murder. No one was charged; and 62 years later, there was a confession stating the accuser had lied on the witness stand about young Emmett accosting her and making inappropriate statements. He, in truth, had only whistled, as his grandfather testified. This heinous hate crime broke the Till family, his Mississippi community and any with a compassionate heart in ways that, even now, no words can explain. Emmett Till's death was a major catalyst for the civil rights movement.

The injustices on people of color must cease. This is unacceptable. How do we counsel and comfort young Black men, women and children who do not feel safe in their communities when all they see are actions produced from a long history of racism, hatred, violence and killing of people of color? My journey of experiencing and exploring injustices has been hard, and it is but one of the many stories of people who are also tired of such injustices. I hope my story serves a purpose for other artists who use their creativity to inspire change.

Following the murder of Michael Brown and protests from the Ferguson, St. Louis and national communities, we found a lot of tension and hatred for police officers. Police brutality toward people of color continues to dominate the headlines. Today, the public's view of law enforcement is largely negative, as it was in 2014. Police brutality and self-proclaimed law enforcement have caused the senseless deaths of many: George Floyd, Breonna Taylor, Ahmaud Arbery, Trayvon Martin, Tamir Rice, Michael Brown, Eric Garner, Philando Castile, Sandra Bland, Ezell Ford, Dante Parker, Michelle Cusseaux, Natasha McKenna, Anthony Hill, Alteria Woods, Terence Crutcher, Michael Lorenzo Dean, Eric Reason, Aaron Bailey, Botham Jean, Pamela Turner, Alton Sterling, Bettie Jones, Troy Robinson, Peter Gaines, Freddie Gray and Dominique Clayton, and that is just to name the people who have captured our attention on the national level. Our communities of color have continued to be traumatized and re-traumatized throughout history.

Over the past four years, relationships with other professional collaborators have been created in tandem with the *Antigone in Ferguson* project to provide multiple layers of services, such as counseling, support from the Brooklyn Public Library (resources) and community engagement opportunities for our thousands of audience members, as a supplement to the show itself. Having been thrust into this social justice arts piece and as a creator of a music project that addresses oppression, I have been able to contribute to this movement for social change in our communities of color by providing an artistic platform which provokes important conversations surrounding these crucial issues.

Benjamin Lloyd Crump is an American civil rights attorney whom we have come to trust when facing the unlawful killing of children of color. In his book, *Open Season, Legalized Genocide of Colored People,* Crump makes a call to action for Americans to begin living up to the promise to protect the rights of citizens equitably without question.

The arts have a history of providing healing and positivity in communities experiencing pain for people of all races, backgrounds, socioeconomic status, sexual orientations and political views[38]. Building the first choir for *Antigone in Ferguson* was a testament to my life's work in the diverse music community of St. Louis. I shared some of the different aspects of my music career in the beginning of this book to give details on how this very unique ensemble of singers and musicians was created. As I reflect on my choice of soloists, it is amazing to see all the perfect roles they have played in my life and in the show. De-Rance Blaylock has supported my work in the arts since I was 18 years old at Saint Louis University and is now the touring superstar of this production. Meeting Detective John Leggette during the early days of the police choir led to a good and loyal friendship, and now he has added so much to this *Antigone in Ferguson* project as well. Our Broadway star, Duane Foster, was an obvious choice. Duane's prestigious career alone, not to mention his connections to Normandy High School and Michael Brown, brought significance to this process. Furthermore, Duane's tenacity and candid rhetoric added

---

[38] Horowitz, S. (2013). The healing power of music and dance. *Alternative and Complementary Therapies, 19*(5), 265-269.https://doi.org/10.1177/1473325010368316

an abundant amount of strength to the production as a whole. If I had not worked closely with Duane the year before on *Memphis*, this task would have been nearly impossible. Finally, Gheremi Clay is one of the most talented Black men with whom I have ever worked during my time in St. Louis. His natural approach to acting and his beautiful vocal ability complete the powerhouse storytelling team for this show.

One serendipitous outcome from this production was the music community that germinated within the choir throughout the rehearsal and performance process. This tight-knit community showed the many audiences who witnessed the power of *Antigone in Ferguson*, the power of love and acceptance. The positive vibes of the choir would spread into the audience members and take root in the hearts and spirits of the audiences who participated in these exercises.

The design of the project itself is arranged to allow the Greek chorus of the play to respond to the action happening on stage boldly throughout the play. During the rehearsal process, I challenged the chorus to consider themselves ambassadors of the project and agents for social change for the audience members in attendance at each performance. While my responsibility as the choir leader was to inspire the chorus members through this rehearsal process, the chorus's role was to inspire the audiences each night with their interpretation of the music and text. Therefore, this core choir (which I called a "team of ambassadors") worked with the director and the creative team to help guide the sensitive conversations, about systemic racism, race relations, police brutality and political injustices, that occurred each night. The core choir took up these leadership roles in order to delve deep into these difficult topics with each other and also to compel audience members to contemplate these topics during post-performance discussions and after the show. This was accomplished during the post-performance conversations when chorus members expressed their own thoughtful views and experiences that the project had impacted. These staged models, along with the moderated post-performance conversations, were used to empower audiences to speak their truths. It took dedicated effort from this entire team to make this process successful each night.

The gospel music before the play started was an outlet for the singers to connect with one another and an invitation to the audiences of *Antigone in Ferguson* to enter an inviting space where art was actively being presented as they were finding their seats. This decision was affirmed by some audience members who shared they heard the gospel music from the street, wanted to know what was happening inside and therefore, came in to find out. During the run at the St. Ann and Holy Trinity Episcopal Church in Brooklyn, New York, a woman stood to share that she was driving by the church in her Uber™ and told the driver to stop, so she and her family could come in and see what was going on in this church, hearing the choir singing the pre-show music from the street. Several shared during the post-show discussion that they were just walking by and wanted to know what was happening.

One of the most special moments occurred when a woman in the audience, who had been feverishly looking for a notary to sign her documents, shared about her Saturday. After the first place she'd looked for a notary turned out to be a bust, she was directed in the opposite direction, leading her to pass the church where our production was in progress. As she was approaching, she said the music sounded so good that she decided to stop in and sit in the back of the church for just a short while, even though she knew her information needed to be notarized that day. She stayed for the remainder of the show and post-show discussion and told her story to the audience. Of course, one of our VIP guests on the first row stood and said she was a notary. Mission accomplished, with a musical play in-between. Again, this was evidence that our plan, "the doors of the church are always open," worked much better than needing a ticket for a reserved seat. We heard from the old and the young, all sharing their stories in a special way. These, and many other stories and experiences during this process, were direct confirmations to me that the music and its performance created a power that gave a voice to the silenced and the soft spoken, power to the downtrodden and hope to the discouraged heart.

As a result of the many performances of *Antigone in Ferguson* in different cities, venues, and settings, along with the research conducted on this project, a model to support this experience has been developed.

Specifically, this includes engaging the chorus in this process of examining issues of racism, even when rehearsal time is limited. I view this rehearsal process as a training time for the chorus as much as a music rehearsing, providing opportunities for them to observe and understand the *Antigone in Ferguson* model and the importance of being mentally present during this process. This model also allowed me to help the chorus adopt a mindset toward change, personal growth and openness to diverse perspectives as well as demonstrate and advocate for democracy. Additionally, I am able to facilitate thoughtful and healing conversation along with music making.

Often in the media, we only hear one part of the story. One major topic discussed in our post-performance audience conversations is the delusion of "fake news" and how the media shapes society's thinking in so many ways. Our presuppositional bias forces us to consider what we experience in a monochromatic way. In other words, everyone has a lens through which they view life. Such a lens is colored by their experiences. Two people may see the same canvas and still have the same response of awestruck beauty. Not a word needs to be spoken for both to understand they are having a similar reaction. However, without any more discussion, both may assume they had the same response for the same reason. It is only in the discussion, following the experience, that the true beauty of the painting comes forth. Without conversation, both are deprived of aspects of beauty that cannot be understood on their own.

Furthermore, in the post-performance discussion, a level of vulnerability is needed to allow for people to explore an intimate space in a thoughtful and productive way. Trying to force vulnerability by providing too much structure can register as inauthentic. In other words, give just enough stimulus to provide a framework whereby the audience fills in the details with their own subconscious, then surprising the subconscious by abruptly focusing on the genuine inspiration. Sharing the details provides an authentic and unique atmosphere seldom experienced, not only individually but corporately. Since vulnerability follows vulnerability, communal thought processing and discovery are accomplished through a passing of the microphone. There is great potential for healing through vulnerability because, through the differences in perspective, the similarities can be appreciated.

Hopefully, the production inspires audience members to go share the "good news" of *Antigone in Ferguson* with others. Even before we take the stage to share our story, the choir members already have a bond that cannot be broken. This infectious energy and unity from the choir has been shared with audiences all over the country. We hope that, as a creative team, our audiences then transfer that energy and unity back into their homes and neighborhoods.

The impact of this production has stretched much further than we ever could have imagined. We have served thousands since 2016. If each of those individuals spread the word about our production to five more people and then those five come to see the production, a cycle begins to occur. If all that have seen the production share the "good news" of *Antigone in Ferguson* with five others to spark conversations in their communities surrounding these important topics, then we can begin to effect change throughout the country and the world. These honest and healing conversations are critical to finding a way forward for our nation.

Black, Brown and White Americans need to openly and honestly work together toward the same goals. This means eradicating the structures that promote White privilege and White power, and developing an agenda that will bring a measure of peace on earth and goodwill to all mankind in America. Now is the time to discuss real equality, implement real change and write new laws to override the Jim Crow-like laws. This change will only be effective if it starts at the top. Dismantling systems of oppression, removing corrupt leadership, providing therapy and counsel for mental health (i.e. Michelle Cusseaux) and closing the economic gap between the poorest and richest communities are just a few burning issues with which we must grapple. Speaking the universal language of love can begin and perpetuate forward momentum.

After the great success of *Antigone in Ferguson* touring the country, yet another opportunity to compose arose when Bryan came to me with another production, pitching the idea that we would leave the world of Greek tragedy and take on an iconic speech by the great

Dr. Martin Luther King, Jr. entitled, "The Drum Major Instinct." It is the final sermon Dr. Martin Luther King, Jr. delivered to his congregation at Ebenezer Baptist Church in Atlanta, Georgia, exactly two months before he was assassinated. Bryan asked if I would take this sermon and create the same style of performance as *Antigone in Ferguson.*

I listened to the sermon and printed a transcript to read so that I could envision how I would incorporate music with these great words. After a third reading of the sermon text, I then started developing main themes and subjects that I thought my music would complement the text. After a few think-tank sessions and some lyric writing forums with Teese, I finalized the lyrics and began working on the songs.

Just like *Antigone in Ferguson,* Bryan decided to partner with Brooklyn Information & Culture (BRIC), a leading arts and media institution in Brooklyn, New York, for a premiere that was a mere seven weeks away from when we agreed to create this show. With such a successful model for *Antigone in Ferguson,* I kept things similar. However, this time, I decided upon a true gospel style throughout the show to be in the spirit of the sermon. I built the same choir and band for this project, as I did in St. Louis, and reached out to Marcelle in New York to collaborate with her choir again on this premiere. For this production, I decided to frame the show around James Cleveland's gospel power ballad, "God Is," led by soloists, Lita Taylor and Debbie Jones who made the song their own and did a tremendous job of guiding the audience into this show with the right spirit.

This presented a new challenge because I wasn't able to teach any of the music in my head to the choir in New York in-person until performance weekend, leaving me with the only option of sending practice tracks and phone calls to prepare. Even with all of the challenges presented, *The Drum Major Instinct,* starring Samira Wiley and Jumaane Williams, New York City Public Advocate, splitting the role of Dr. King, was a smash hit and grew some traction across the country.

The Drum Major Instinct toured the country to many college campuses and institutions and also premiered in Athens, Greece, at the

Stavros Niarchos Foundation international annual conference in Kallithea, one year after *Antigone in Ferguson*. Even though I never thought we would be asked back to Greece twice in two years, it was a tremendous opportunity to return to Greece a second time to perform a work celebrating Black culture. It has been an awe-inspiring journey sharing these two incredible shows with the world since 2016.

Another takeaway from this story was the gift of composition that was revealed to me during this process. My experience in composition before this project consisted of only a few gospel numbers for a CD project (that was never released) for Melody of Praise Gospel Ensemble, Saint Louis University's Gospel Choir, and a three-part choral number I wrote as tribute to my eighth-grade singers one year during our final concert. Even with one class in composition, I lacked the confidence in my skill-level to compose an entire production's lyrics and music; however, I put into practice the lessons I've learned, and I listened to those who have faith and trust in me.

In addition to the work at my father's church, I have programmed gospel choirs in St. Louis for years, organizing and directing several anniversary mass choirs for New Hope Baptist Church, First Baptist Church of Chesterfield and Pleasant Green Baptist Church. In addition to my mass choir work, I have organized and conducted a few full concerts: Fee Fee Baptist Church's Summer Gospel Choir Series, Phil Woodmore and Friends; a series of concerts at Northern Arizona University for a two-year residency with the university and the State of Arizona, as well as a gospel choir collaboration with the state of Arizona, the NAU Gospel Choir and the Phil Woodmore Singers of St. Louis. In 2019, I held my first gospel music workshop at Washington Metropolitan AME Zion Church, where Duane Foster, minister of music, asked me to write music for his workshop and then teach that music to the participants for a concert.

In 2018, I made the tough decision to resign as the choir director at Crestview Middle School to pursue working with Theater of War Productions and *Antigone in Ferguson* full time. It took me a long time to come to terms and be at peace with this decision, similarly to the guilt I experienced when leaving the Ferguson-Florissant students in 2006. I felt like a traitor leaving the Ferguson-Florissant students; however, I had quickly learned there were students of color in Rockwood who needed me as well. Additionally, the White students in my school needed me more than I even knew. Coming back to Rockwood, the district I attended as a youth, now as an educator, I found my place as a mentor and counselor to many of my students dealing with depression, homelessness, suicidal thoughts, witnessing murder, violence in the home and other terrible issues young people should not have to experience. And to my surprise, many of these conversations were with my White students. Children are children, regardless of race—they all need love and a shoulder to lean on in tough times.

Beyond my efforts at Crestview, I also learned that holding a position of power as a man of color de-centers Whiteness and replaces it with diversity in thinking. For some White community members, my position as a Black choir teacher was a new normal, as it served to problematize any notions of supremacy and self-importance. However, just as I had to prove myself in the Ferguson Florissant School District with the many Black faculty and families, I did feel I had to prove myself in Rockwood with the many White faculty and families as well. But I decided along the way that I needed to be me. I made a commitment to all my students when taking the position at CMS, to get them all through choir class and to the finish line as successful learners, as they moved on to high school. I am a Black man—before I get to school, during teaching and after I leave. I chose to be myself and not change my ways of speaking, acting or living to conform to someone else's vision for me as a middle school choir teacher.

I made so many special connections with many families and faculty members in the district that I will always hold dear to my heart during my time in Rockwood. I am an educator of all people. I love all people; and I want to see all people learn and succeed. I eventually realized that as I left my classroom, I was not abandoning my students that I had grown to love. Instead, I was transitioning from a local middle school classroom to a national and international classroom with even more people to teach and love.

I may no longer be teaching my 350 middle school students, but I am now educating people across the nation through the art of music, its practice, performance and important conversations about social justice matters in our broken society. With the growing stress and chaos of the coronavirus pandemic and the ever-evolving racial pandemic that is now opening the eyes of some and re-traumatizing others, the healing arts are more important than ever. Arts and arts education construct a platform for people to express their feelings in a creative, healthy and unique way that cannot be accomplished in other forums. The 2020 pandemic added to the gaping hole that already existed in our society and world by causing the shutdown of many institutions, including the arts institutions. While all are treading upon unknown territory with added political intrusion, I trust science and wait hopefully that our theatrical seats will soon be filled again.

Please support artists and arts institutions—without an arts education and artists' mentors growing up, *Antigone in Ferguson* would not exist, and this needed production would still be an idea or exist in a different and possibly ineffective form.

Music unites countless people. New York City Sergeant Marcus Lewis stated in his interview for my research project that, "*Antigone in Ferguson* speaks the universal language of music." He elaborated that the arts bring people together. The arts can be transformative and used to change people's thinking, in a positive way, through the exercise of *Antigone in Ferguson*. As we work to bring the arts projects into more virtual forums, please support these efforts and give space for artists to create. The world will look much different if the arts do not come back as a strong force in our society; therefore, we must do everything in our power to keep this from happening.

Now it's your turn. "What do I do with all of this?" you might ask. Go to work! Get involved in the discussion of discrimination any way you can. I never saw myself on the front lines of a protest, but adding this project to the body of music as activism is my form of protest. I protest with my art. Sharing this with many diverse communities provides a platform to discuss in a nonthreatening way. You might not have the skill set to compose music, but maybe you are an organizer and can get together a peaceful protest or organize a rally to promote justice and equality. Maybe you have neighbors in your community who don't really "get it" whom you can talk to and share insightful information that could redirect their thinking. Or maybe you can speak up when you see injustice in action to help those blinded by tradition to see what's possible. Progress is possible, one human at a time.

If you don't know where to start or you want to learn more, then check out the resources I have compiled in the back of the book to provide some context for these crucial matters and hear from other great thinkers on these topics. Additionally, in honor of the exercise of discussion in *Antigone in Ferguson,* I have also provided some discussion questions to frame conversations you might have surrounding this book and this show. These questions and resources are a very small portion of the great things available to help educate yourself on these matters, but a place to start learning and growing.

Music shares things that go beyond the realm of language. One of the most powerful conversations I had during my time in *Antigone in Ferguson* was with a minister of music, turned pastor, from a church in Queens who shared how moving music was for him. He went on to talk about the universal language of music and how it speaks to all people. He shared how inspired he was to be participating in this show because he had not been challenged musically like this in a long time; even though he felt he couldn't read much of the music that well, he still could feel its power and connect with the messages that I had poured into my writing. This was a prodigious moment for me, as I witnessed the power of music for someone who was not a buttoned-up music scholar, but was a real person who connected with this universal language in such an authentic way. Music is the lifeline for many people and provides a voice for those who might not otherwise be able to express themselves.

All of my experiences in the classroom and vocal coaching had led me to the pinnacle moment in my career of creating and managing the music department of *Antigone in Ferguson.* Even though this show is an amazing experience and opportunity for communities all over the globe to engage in thought-provoking conversations, there is a great amount of musical work that precedes the conversation. Often, I move from music teacher to counselor, as many things discussed in this production are very emotional for some of the chorus members participating. As the music leader/counselor, being able to carefully navigate rehearsals and heart-to-heart conversations is critical to the success of this production. Also, there are many general day-to-day items that have to be addressed in the process of creating a successful choral dynamic—copies of music, rehearsal schedules, locations and times. My life's work has prepared me for a time such as this.

The *Antigone in Ferguson* project serves as a choral/musical theater example that adds to the body of literature about transformative music organizations, such as intergenerational choirs, prison choirs and homeless choirs. The model created has given a tremendous amount of evidence to the power of music and the universal language of art in communities who need to find a way forward. Creating this project from its inception and breathing life into these musical compositions has provided me with a tremendous platform to share the "good news" of *Antigone in Ferguson*. My life's work has come to a zenith moment called *Antigone in Ferguson*; my prayer is that this work will touch the lives of people around the globe in a way that brings change to societies, hope to our youth and promote the message of love to all.

The love of music and justice for all was within me always, innate. *Antigone in Ferguson* brought to the forefront my unforeseen drive and passion that everyone be treated fairly. I wanted to model fairness. I wanted to teach it by my lifestyle. After all, fairly was not that big of a word, or so I thought. God opened my heart and creative mind to compose this project. He gave me the ability to develop what was within, and then He brought the vehicle, *Antigone in Ferguson*, needed to implement His purpose. All my life my father, Pastor Willie Woodmore, has always provided a shoulder to lean on and spiritual guidance in a way that was not forced. I have heard him preach that living in the truth of Jesus Christ leads to liberty (John 8:31-32), and now I find myself seeking after and longing to live in the light of love and liberty of the truth.

Thank God, I'm Covered!

DISCUSSION QUESTIONS

Thank you for taking the time to read this book! Antigone in Ferguson is an important part of my life, and I am so honored to share this experience with you. Below is a list of questions to consider, as starting points for your conversations. I encourage you to allow the conversations to go in whatever direction they are organically moving. It is okay for the conversation to get messy; remember, everyone has their own opinion and is allowed to share from their heart. Hopefully, with more facts and truth, a better understanding will promote change that brings healing to our nation.

Explore—Discuss—Unite!

"The grand words of proud men are punished with great blows.
That is wisdom." ~Antigone in Ferguson

1. Have you seen or experienced institutionalized racism in action in your school, community, job and country? If yes, how do we dissolve this system, and at the same time, promote equality for all people?

2. Black Lives Matter is a movement established in response to the acquittal of Trayvon Martin's murder by George Zimmerman. Their website says join the movement and fight for freedom, liberation and justice. What are your thoughts about the "Black Lives Matter Movement"? https://blacklivesmatter.com/about/

3. How might additional resources (money, personnel, facilities, etc.) be used to solve, resolve or even minimize the killings of citizens by police in many poor communities?

4. Define "defund the police" and "dismantle the police" and how would it apply in your city?

5. Define and/or explain the difference between White privilege and White supremacy? Do either prevail in your school, community, job, leisure activities or other areas? If yes, in what way?

6. After George Floyd and Breonna Taylor's death, the country took a stand against racism and elevated the efforts of Black Lives Matter through peaceful protest and displays across the country. What is the difference between rioting and looting and peaceful protesting?

7. What is allyship? Are there communities that need your public display of allyship?

8. How could we better serve the mentally ill with counseling and/or possibly better equip police officers to address calls concerning the mentally ill?

9. One term that comes up during our post-performance conversation is intersectionality[39]. How does it pertain to the current state of our nation today? How can we use the concept of intersectionality to become aware of our own biases and privileges?

10. What is the final U.S. Citizenship and Immigration Services (USCIS) public charge rule for handling undocumented immigrants? Do you agree or disagree with this rule?

11. What are your takeaways from the story of Antigone in Ferguson? What areas of your life need some attention?

12. After reading this book, are there ways that you could (and maybe should) make changes in your own life to affect change in people around you?

---

[39] **Intersectionality**- theoretical framework coined by Kimberlé Crenshaw which by definition means the interconnected nature of social categorizations such as race, class and gender as they apply to a given individual or group, regarded as creating overlapping and interdependent systems of discrimination or disadvantage.

RESOURCES:
MATTERS OF SOCIAL JUSTICE

<u>Books</u>

Becoming by Michelle Obama

The Blood of Emmett Till by Timothy B. Tyson

How to be an Antiracist by Ibram X. Kendi

Just Mercy: A Story of Justice and Redemption by Bryan Stevenson

The Life, Legacy, and Love of My Son Michael Brown
by Lezley McSpadden-Head

The New Jim Crow: Mass Incarceration in the Age of Colorblindedness
by Michelle Alexander

Open Season by Ben Crump

The President's Devotional by Joshua DuBois

Rest in Power by Sybrina Fulton & Tracy Martin

This Stops Today by Gwen Carr

White Fragility: Why It's So Hard for White People to Talk about Racism
by Robin DiAngelo

White Privilege Unmasked: How to be Part of the Solution by J. Ryde

White Rage: The Unspoken Truth of Our Racial Divide by C. Anderson

If you have children who are interested in learning more about this
topic, listed below are some books specifically for them:

Black Lives Matter by Sue Bradford Edwards

A Wreath for Emmett Till by Marilyn Nelson

A is for Activist by Innosanto Nagara

The Hate You Give by Angie Thomas

Together We Stand Against Racism by Sonja Smith

Web Resources

Alfred C. Sharpton, Jr. National Action Network, President and Founder: https://nationalactionnetwork.net/

Black Lives Matter: https://blacklivesmatter.com/

Center for American Progress: https://www.americanprogress.org/

Emmett Till Legacy Foundation: https://emmetttilllegacyfoundation.com/

Garner Way Foundation (E.R.I.C.) Eliminating Racism Inequality Collectively: http://garnerwayfoundation.org/

Mapping Police Violence: https://mappingpoliceviolence.org

The Michael Brown Chosen for Change Foundation: https://www.facebook.com/MichaelBrownFoundationCFC/

The Michael O. D. Brown, Rainbow of Mothers: We love strengthening and supporting families: http://michaelodbrown.org/index.php/rainbow-of-mothers/

The Michael O. D. Brown, We Love our Sons and Daughters Foundation: http://michaelodbrown.org/

Prison Policy Initiative: https://www.prisonpolicy.org/

Race Forward: https://www.raceforward.org/

The Trayvon Martin Foundation: https://www.trayvonmartinfoundation.org/

GLOSSARY

Alto- the lowest female singing voice, also known as contralto or the highest adult male singing voice, countertenor.

Anthem- 1 - a rousing or uplifting song identified with a particular group, body or cause. 2 - a choral composition based on a biblical passage for singing by a choir in a church service.

Baritone- an adult male singing voice between tenor and bass.

Bass- the lowest adult male singing voice.

Dynamics- how quietly or loudly music should be played.

Fanfare- a short ceremonial tune or flourish played on a brass instrument, typically to introduce something or someone important.

Greek Chorus- a homogeneous, non-individualized group of performers, who comment with a collective voice on the dramatic action in the context of ancient Greek tragedy, comedy, satire and modern works inspired by them.

Homophonic- characterized by the movement of accompanying parts in the same rhythm as the melody. Often contrasted with polyphonic.

Mezzo-Soprano- a female singer with a voice pitched between soprano and contralto.

Oratorio- an extended musical composition with text more or less dramatic in character and usually based on a religious theme for solo voices, chorus and orchestra, and performed with action, costume or scenery.

Pitch- the higher or lower frequency of a single sound/note.

Recitative- musical declamation of the kind usual in the narrative and dialogue parts of opera and oratorio, sung in the rhythm of ordinary speech with many words on the same note.

Soprano- the highest of the four standard singing voices, a female or boy singer with a soprano voice.

Swing Soloist-a member of the company who understudies several chorus and/or dancing roles.

Tenor- a singing voice between baritone and alto or countertenor, the highest of the ordinary adult male range.

Tech-Week- the days used to rehearse a theatrical production with most or all of its elements including lighting, sound, scenery and costumes.

Tessitura- the vocal range within which most notes of a vocal part fall.

Texture- the overall quality of harmonic and melodic layers of sound.

Through-line- a connecting theme, plot or characteristic in a film, television series, book or play.

ORIGINAL
ANTIGONE IN FERGUSON
CHOIR AND BAND

Soprano
De-Andrea Blaylock-
Johnson
Kelli Lowe
Samantha Madison
Elise Oates
Melissa Pickens
Lawanda Smith
Shelia Taylor
Carol Whittier

ALTO
Latricia Allen
Judy Armstrong
De-Rance Blaylock
Debbie Jones
Valeria Walker-Triplett
Mindy Wood-Bates

Tenor/Bass
Tameka Anderson
Gheremi Clay
Arushus Coleman
Robert Crenshaw
Virginia Dulaney-Cane
Duane Foster
Christian Hamilton
Allan Hibbler
Paul Hinton
Lawrence Hudson-Lewis
Ezekiel Jones
John Leggette
Antoine Watkins

Band
Jason Davis
Ja'mes Davis
Bernard Long Jr.
Willie Woodmore

Thank you all for your continued support, as I take this project around the world. I will never forget your dedication to this important process and the sacrifice you all made to make *Antigone in Ferguson* a stamp on history.
Bravo!

ORIGINAL ANTIGONE IN FERGUSON HARLEM CHOIR

Soprano
Sarah Hopp
Jasmine Muhammad

Alto
Tamera Fingal
Jhetti Lashley
Marcelle Davies-Lashley

Tenor/Bass
Jonathan Elkins
Marcus Lewis
Daniel McRath
Stacy Penson

Special shout to these amazing singers who helped carry the *Antigone in Ferguson* torch in our 30-show Off-Broadway DEBUT! **Job well done!**

ORIGINAL
ANTIGONE IN FERGUSON
BROOKLYN CHOIR AND BAND

Soprano
Sheherazade Holman
Diamond Jones
Briana Sheriff

Alto
Carolynn Clynn
Madeleine Ledu

Tenor/Bass
Jovon Davis
Shaq Hester
Elijah London
Terrol Stone

Band
Fred Cash
Anna Dagmar
Henry Keys
Etienne Lashley
Lee Odom

These extraordinary singers and musicians continued the spirit of
Antigone in Ferguson in the 50-show run in Brooklyn—
Couldn't have done it without YOU!

AUTHOR'S NOTES

Additional Resources by the Author:

Study Guide: A Closer Look at Justice is an additional teaching tool for *Antigone in Ferguson: A Journey Through the Transformative Power of Music.* Continue the conversation! This study guide provides more in-depth discussion questions and a wealth of information about the topic of justice that will hopefully inform you and your study group on current events. To purchase and download the study guide (offered in the Teacher Edition of this book), visit www.philipawoodmore.com and go to the STORE tab.

Tragedy to Triumph: Bible Study is a comprehensive bible study for study groups interested in exploring themes from this show from a biblical lens. Greek tragedies are characterized by people facing serious dilemmas in life who make grossly wrong decisions that result in devastating consequences with no hope of deliverance. The gospel of Jesus Christ on the other hand addresses people who have also made grossly wrong decisions with devastating consequences, but offers hope of complete and thorough deliverance (Romans 1:16). For this reason, the gospel is "good news." So regardless of your past, the gospel offers light, love, liberty and eternal life! To purchase and download *Tragedy to Triumph*, please visit www.philipawoodmore.com and go to the STORE tab.

To continue the conversation and stay updated, please subscribe to the mailing list on my website: www.philipawoodmore.com for a newsletter with upcoming performances, more information on *Antigone in Ferguson* and a free download of a lyrics packet for all of the songs.

ABOUT THE AUTHOR

Saint Louis native, Dr. Philip A. Woodmore has been an active member of the St. Louis music community for many years. Phil received his bachelors from Saint Louis University in Business Marketing and Music Vocal Performance, his masters from Webster University in Music Education, and his PhD in Music Education from the University of Missouri-Columbia. His research interests are the changing voice, voice pedagogy, and the transformative power of music. His dissertation is on the transformative power of music in the choral setting using the auditioned choir in the Off-Broadway run of Antigone in Ferguson. Phil taught choir one year at Ferguson and Berkley Middle Schools in the Ferguson-Florissant School District and then went on to become the choir director at Crestview Middle School in the Rockwood School District where he taught for 12 years. Along with his work in Rockwood, Phil was the Coordinator of the Voice Program at the Center of Creative Arts (COCA) and the artist director of the Allegro Music Company from 2008-2017, has been the director of the Saint Louis Metropolitan Police Department Choir since 2009, was the director of the Northern Arizona University Gospel Choir from 2014-2017, Artist in Residency for the State of Arizona for a two year term 2016-2018, minister of music at Trinity Community Church from 1992-2018, and vocal coach to many in the St. Louis and New York areas.

In August 2016 Phil was asked to compose an original score of a version of Antigone, translated by Bryan Doerries, called *Antigone in Ferguson. Antigone in Ferguson* has been traveling the country for the past four years and premiered internationally in Athens, Greece in June 2016. Since the success of Antigone in Ferguson, Phil has written an original score for Dr. Martin Luther King Jr.'s last sermon, *The Drum Major Instinct* and also for a speech by Frederick Douglass. Phil joined the Muny family for the 2020 summer season and he is looking forward to a great partnership as the Music Director for Muny Kids. For more information on Dr. Philip A. Woodmore please visit www.philipawoodmore.com

Printed in the USA
CPSIA information can be obtained
at www.ICGtesting.com
LVHW021929071123
763306LV00005B/118